CULTURES OF THE WORLD®

ROMANIA

Sean Sheehan

BENCHMARK BOOKS

MARSHALL CAVENDISH
NEW YORK

PICTURE CREDITS
Cover photo: © Alamy Images: Robert Harding World Imagery
alt.TYPE/REUTERS: 34, 35, 50 • ANA Press Agency: 54 • Camera Press: 16, 57, 77 • Coca-Cola (Gerhard Hinterleitner): 42 • Corbis Inc.: 52, 53 • Embassy of Romania (Singapore): 60, 98, 111, 112, 129 • Focus Team Italy: 16, 28, 46, 49, 96 • George Enescu Orchestra: 97 • Getty Images: 33 • HBL Network Photo Agency: 5, 36, 66 • Hepta Photo Agency: 123 • Hulton-Deutsch Collection: 11, 12, 13, 20, 22, 23, 24, 26, 40, 41, 44, 45, 65, 67, 110, 114, 115, 117 • Hutchison Library: 3, 4, 37, 39, 43, 55, 76, 84, 91, 101, 105, 118, 126, 128 • Image Bank: 7, 59 • Impact Photos: 68, 70, 71, 72, 73, 74, 93, 122 • Interfoto MTI: 8, 121 • Bjorn Klingwall: 1, 19, 91, 98, 113 • Life File Photo Library: 18, 30, 38, 58, 61, 69, 79, 86, 89, 95, 102, 103, 109 • Lonely Planet Images: 48 • Reuters Visnews: 15 • STOCKFOOD/FOODFOTO KOLN: 131 • STOCKFOOD/FOODPHOTOGR. EISING: 130 • Sylvia Cordaiy Photo Library: 78, 108 • Liba Taylor: 14, 64, 75, 80, 118

ACKNOWLEDGMENTS
Thanks to Holly Case of the Department of History at Cornell University for her expert reading of this manuscript. Thanks to Mr. Sever Cotu, Charge D'Affaires A.I. & Minister Counselor, Embassy of Romania, Singapore, for his assistance.

PRECEDING PAGE
Romanian schoolboys pose before a statue of Protestant reformer Johannes Honterus in Brasov city.

Marshall Cavendish Benchmark
99 White Plains Road
Tarrytown, NY 10591
Website: www.marshallcavendish.us

Originated and designed by Times Editions
An imprint of Marshall Cavendish International (Asia) Private Limited
A member of Times Publishing Limited

Library of Congress Cataloging-in-Publication Data
Sheehan, Sean, 1951-
    Romania / by Sean Sheehan.
        p. cm. — (Cultures of the world)
    Summary: "Explores the geography, history, government, economy, people, and culture
        of Romania"—Provided by publisher.
    Includes bibliographical references and index.
    ISBN 0-7614-1848-2
    1. Romania—Juvenile literature. I. Title. II. Series.
    DR205.S48 200
    949.8—dc22   2004027507

Printed in China

7 6 5 4 3 2 1

CONTENTS

A Romanian man from Maramures County.

Villagers gather for the annual agricultural fair in Botiza in Transylvania.

INTRODUCTION

THE NAME OF ROMANIA, a country in southeastern Europe, means land of the Romans. Romanians are proud of the fact that they can trace their language and ethnic identity back to the days of the ancient Roman Empire. Romania has endured centuries of struggle against enemies from beyond its borders and, more recently, from its own fascist and Communist governments that nearly ruined the country and almost eradicated minority cultures.

Romania still faces many problems early in the 21st century, but things are beginning to look better for its long-suffering people. The economy is slowly expanding. Unemployment and inflation rates have fallen. Membership in the European Union promises bigger markets, new business opportunities, and greater foreign investment. The Romanian government is paying more attention to improving social services and the environment. Democracy in Romania may still be in its infancy, and the people may still be wary of their political leaders, but now at least the people are free to celebrate their rich and diverse culture.

GEOGRAPHY

ROMANIA IS SITUATED in the southeast of Europe, at the northern part of the Balkan Peninsula. It lies between latitudes 43°N and 48°N and longitudes 20°E and 29°E. The area of Romania is 91,700 square miles (237,500 square km), and it is a little smaller than the state of Oregon. It is bounded on the north and northeast by Ukraine and Moldova; on the northwest by Hungary; on the southeast and south by the Black Sea and Bulgaria; and on the southwest by Serbia and Montenegro (formerly known as Yugoslavia).

About 31 percent of the country is covered by the Carpathian Mountains, which form a series of crescents around the large Transylvanian Basin, a plateau in the west of the country. Beyond the mountain ranges to the south and east, the mighty Danube River and its tributaries enrich extensive plains that make up 36 percent of the country.

Left: **Cattle crossing the lower stretch of the Danube River. The river sustains a wide range of agricultural activities in the Walachian region, including dairy farming.**

Opposite: **The village of Botiza is located in the mountainous region of Maramures in northwestern Romania.**

The steep and rugged walls of the Turda canyon in the Transylvanian Alps were formed by glacial erosion.

CARPATHIAN MOUNTAINS

The Carpathian Mountains form part of the great alpine uplift that was created 50 to 65 million years ago during the Tertiary period. They stretch for some 700 miles (1,800 km) on Romanian territory, forming a curve around Transylvania, and then separating into three main ranges. The highest range, the Southern Carpathians, is commonly known as the Transylvanian Alps because of the many glacial features found there. A typical feature is a cirque, a steep-sided hollow caused by glacial erosion, which is usually found at the head of a mountain valley. Many cirques have been carved into the sides of the Transylvanian Alps. There are also many beautiful glacial lakes, a testimony to the last Ice Age. The highest point in the country, Mount Moldoveanu at 8,346 feet (2,544 m), is found in the Alps.

The Eastern Carpathians include zones of sandstone ridges, limestone formations, and volcanic ranges. Imposing river gorges wind their way through these mountains, flanked by limestone walls that reach heights of over 300 feet (91.4 m). The volcanic zone, composed mainly of long-dead craters and cones, is heavily forested with commercial plantations of conifer trees.

The Western Carpathians are the lowest in elevation and contain many of the largest caves in the country. Evidence of human habitation going back to the Stone Age has been found in mountain caves in Romania. Unlike the other two Carpathian ranges, the Western Carpathians are not a continuous range. They are characterized by clusters of mountains in a

CARPATHIAN HIGHLIGHTS

Most of the Carpathian Mountains are composed of hard crystalline and volcanic rocks, but there are also mountainous regions composed of limestone and granite, which make them more susceptible to erosion. Bizarrely shaped rock formations, mighty gorges, and spectacular river valleys have developed, giving the mountains a fascinating appeal for both geologists and tourists.

Another effect of erosion is the number of caves found in the Southern Carpathians (*right*). The caves were formed as a result of water percolating through limestone, forming underground channels and rivers that eventually flow to the surface. Such a landscape is known as karst. Erosion under the surface continues, and intricate cave systems develop as a result.

The science and practice of cave exploration—called speleology—started with a Romanian, Emil Racovita, who established the first speleological institute at a university in the northwest of the Southern Carpathians. Romania's largest ice cavern has a solid block of ice measuring some 60 feet (18.3 m) thick. A favorite tourist attraction, it is found in the Southern Carpathians at the base of a vertical entrance over 160 feet (48.8 m) high. Visitors usually wind their way through the dark interior with the aid of lamps to reach the vaulted central cavern, where ice columns and limestone structures are found.

north-south direction, separated by deep gorges. These gorges have served as strategically important sites, or gates, for gaining access to or defending the region. This function is reflected in their names, like the famous Iron Gate on the Danube.

The mountains provide some of the most attractive scenery Romania has to offer. This, plus the wealth of wildlife, helps explain why the first national parks in Romania were established in the Southern Carpathians in the 1930s. One of the biggest, the Retezat National Park, covers an area of more than 94,016 acres (38,047 hectares) and includes over 80 lakes of glacial origin.

FLORA AND FAUNA

Romania is home to a great diversity of flora and fauna. In the Retezat National Park in the Southern Carpathians, for example, more than 1,200 species of plants have been recorded. Mountainous areas, densely covered with woods, are inhabited by animals like the brown bear and wild boar, which are becoming increasingly rare in other parts of Europe. Quite common in the Southern Carpathians, above the tree line, is the mountain goat known as the chamois. A soft leather obtained from the skin of the chamois makes a good-quality polishing cloth.

Some of the most exciting wildlife is found in the Danube delta region, where millions of birds spend the winter or stop over during their annual migrations. The delta is equidistant from the equator and the North Pole, and makes a natural resting and feeding point for birds before they fly on to northern Europe, China, Siberia, and parts of Africa. Consequently, the Danube delta is rich in the diversity of bird and animal species, and some 300 bird species arrive on a regular basis. Visitors include the Egyptian vulture, the black-winged stilt roller, and the pygmy cormorant.

The upper reaches of the delta, where the water does not cover everything, provide a home to a variety of mammals, such as the mink, muskrat, fox, and wild cat. Various snakes, many of them poisonous, live in colonies on some of the larger islands. In addition, there are about 30 species of bats found across the land, 22 of which live within the country's 85 caves.

The Danube delta is 1,950 square miles (5,050 square km) in area, of which 1,750 square miles (4,532 square km) are in Romania. It has been designated a United Nations Educational, Scientific, and Cultural Organization (UNESCO) biosphere reserve.

FLATLANDS

Flatlands, or plateaus, are elevated areas of land that are often flat on the surface and bounded by steep sides. Most of Transylvania is a large plateau enclosed by the arc of the Carpathian Mountains. Large deposits of methane gas, first exploited over 60 years ago, provide the region with its most valuable resource and makes the plateau one of Romania's most prosperous regions. Many salt lakes and hot springs are found in the Transylvanian Basin, giving rise to numerous spas and health resorts.

Beyond the mountains are more flatlands. To the east of the Eastern Carpathians, in the northeast of Romania, is the Moldavian plateau. This is an important area for grain and sugar beet production, and the steep hills are mined for their granite and quartz.

The part of Romania that lies between the Danube and the Black Sea, called Dobrogea (DOH-bro-jah), also has a plateau formed from eroded rock. The average altitude here is 820 feet (250 m), and while there is little potential for agriculture because of the hot and dry climate, the quarrying of granite is a major activity.

THE PLAINS

Plains are areas of flat or gently rolling ground often formed by deposits from rivers, glaciers, or the sea. They form about one-third of Romania's landmass and characterize much of the land in the south, in the region known as Walachia (Va-LAH-hiah). The Olt River, which runs from the north to the south through the

Harvesting corn in the former Lipove Agricultural Production Cooperative in Arad County. Corn is grown extensively throughout Romania, where it is an important staple food.

southern part of the country, divides the Walachian plain in two. West of the Olt River is the Oltenian plain, which reaches a maximum elevation of 984 feet (300 m), while east of the river lies an area called the Romanian plain. The plains are covered by loess, wind-blown deposits of silt that make very fertile farmland if there is adequate rainfall or irrigation. Romanian farmers depend on dams for irrigation. Farther south, nearer the Danube River, former marshland has been drained, and the rich alluvial soil is suited for crops such as rice and tomatoes. The Walachian plains serve as the granary of the country, where vast fields of wheat and corn produce food for the majority of Romanians.

Above: **Romanian caviar is one of the best in the world. Sturgeon, from which caviar is obtained, was once found in abundance in the Danube River. Its numbers have since declined due to pollution, overfishing, and poaching.**

Opposite: **The 20,000-volts transformer station at the Iron Gate hydropower station.**

THE DANUBE DELTA

The triangular Danube delta, where the river runs into the Black Sea in the southeast of the country, is formed by three tributaries of the Danube River. The area that now makes up the delta was once a bay that, over thousands of years, became filled with mud and sediment carried by the waters of the Danube.

The delta's economic importance is derived from its rich potential for fishing. Half the country's fish come from the delta, which is rich in carp and supplies 90 percent of the sturgeon catch. The eggs of the female sturgeon are used to make caviar, an expensive food considered to have a superior taste to other roe.

The delta has many floating reed islands, formed by large and small collections of reeds rooted together by their rhizomes. The reeds serve an economic purpose. They are harvested, pulped, and then the cellulose content is used for making paper and textiles.

Because the delta-building process is ongoing, the land annually moves several yards into the Black Sea. Approximately 13 to 16 percent of the delta is made up of dry land that is covered by softwood forests, shrubs, and woody vines, which help to give the delta a tropical appearance.

THE POWER OF THE DANUBE

The Danube River is one of the world's mightiest rivers. It is the second longest in Europe, and carries an average of 50 million tons of alluvial deposits every year. It begins in Germany's Black Forest and flows through Austria, Hungary, Serbia, and Ukraine; forms parts of the southern border with both Serbia and Bulgaria; then enters Romania and meanders sluggishly to the Black Sea. The Danube's 668-mile (1,075-km) course through Romania to the Black Sea is completely navigable. For countless centuries, the river was a natural barrier in the south of Romania because of its tremendous width of over 2 miles (3.2 km). Between A.D. 103 and 105, under orders from the emperor Trajan, the Romans constructed a bridge across the Danube at the town of Drobeta-Turnu Severin, which is located in southern Romania.

A few miles upstream from Drobeta-Turnu Severin lies a huge hydroelectric dam to harness the power of the Danube as it flows through the rapids of the Iron Gate that separates Romania and Serbia. The dam, incorporating an international road crossing, was conceived in the 1950s as a joint project between the governments of Romania and Serbia. It was finally completed in 1971. Since the completion of the dam and its lock gates, the rapids of the Iron Gate no longer present a formidable hazard to navigators. But upstream, the Kazan Gorge remains a spectacular and daunting phenomenon. There the river flows fast, twisting and turning as it gushes through a narrow gorge with cliffs over 2,000 feet (610 m) high.

Most of Romania's other rivers are tributaries of the Danube. All tributaries—the Olt, Jiu, Arges, and Ialomita—flow across the plains of Walachia. The second longest river, the Mures, flows westward into Hungary, where it joins another tributary of the great Danube.

CLIMATE

Romania's climate is a temperate continental one, with hot summers and cold winters. The average temperature in July is 70°F (21°C), while in January it drops to slightly below freezing. Icy winds sweep down from Russia in winter, and widespread snowfall is common. Variations in altitude, however, account for regional differences. The plains are always warmer than the mountainous areas, and precipitation—rain and snowfall —can reach 40 inches (101 cm) in the mountains, twice that of the plains. Generally speaking, the climate is well suited for agriculture.

CITIES

The cities of Romania are a mixture of the ancient and the modern.

BUCHAREST The capital of Romania, Bucharest, is situated between the Carpathians and the Danube, in a region once called Walachia. First mentioned in a 15th-century document, it is now home to nearly 2.3 million inhabitants. In its heyday between World War I and World War II, the capital was known as the Paris of the East, but since then it has lost much of its appeal. In many areas of the city, houses dating back to the 18th century were demolished and replaced by modern civic structures

Nearly 20 percent of the country's industrial output is produced in Bucharest, and 9 percent of the population lives there in an area of 587 square miles (1,521 square km).

in the 1970s and 1980s. Rebuilding ceased after 1989, and international loans have helped Bucharest restore and bring life back to historic parts of the city.

BRASOV Brasov was founded by the medieval Saxons in Transylvania and still retains the old streets and buildings that evoke its Gothic past. However, in the years after 1945, thousands of villagers from Moldova settled in Brasov. Factories and blocks of apartments were built and the city is now an industrial center with around 300,000 people.

Textiles, food products, light industries producing farm machinery and electrical equipment, and the oil and chemical industries provide employment for many of the inhabitants. Brasov is also a winter sports center and resort.

Above: **Founded by the Teutonic Knights from Germany in 1211, Brasov was first mentioned in historical documents in 1251.**

Opposite: **Winters are very cold in Romania. Cold northeasterly winds known as the *crivat* blow in from the Russian plains, while air masses from the Black Sea bring in rain and warm air.**

CONSTANTA Constanta on the Black Sea coast is almost as large as Brasov. It has important commercial and transportation links to the capital, which lies about 165 miles (265 km) to the east. Constanta is Romania's major seaport—well over 50 percent of the country's exports pass through its port facilities—and it is the second biggest commercial center on the Black Sea. The city is also developing into an industrial center with packaging, food processing, shipbuilding, and metallurgical industries.

HISTORY

FOR NEARLY 2,000 YEARS, Romania's history was one of conquest and rule by foreign empires. It was only in 1877 that the united principalities of Walachia and Moldavia were formally recognized as an independent state, known as Romania. Even after independence, the history of present-day Romania—consisting of Walachia, Moldavia, and Transylvania—was clouded by a sense of oppression. In 1989, when its own dictatorship was overthrown, the country began a radical new era.

DACIA AND THE ROMANS

When the Romans moved into what is now Romania in A.D. 101, they were conquering a region the ancient Greeks knew as Getae, but was called Dacia by the Romans. The Greeks had established colonies along the Black Sea, but since they never moved inland, Greek culture made little impact on the local population.

The Dacians became subjects of the Roman Empire in A.D. 106. Barely 200 years later, between A.D. 271 to 275, Emperor Aurelian ordered the withdrawal of troops and administrators from the province because of the increasing cost of defending the region from barbarian tribes—a variety of Goths, Huns, Slavs, Avars, Cumans, and Mongols. Despite their short time in Dacia, the Romans had a significant and continuing impact. It is believed that some Roman settlers remained and married the Dacians, who adopted Roman customs and the Latin language. Early forms of Christianity were introduced when Christianity became the official religion of the Roman Empire in the fourth century.

Above: **A carving on Emperor Trajan's column in Rome shows Romans carrying away the Dacian treasury. A replica of Trajan's column is found in the Bucharest museum.**

Opposite: **The remnants of the Princely Court in Targoviste, built in the 14th century. Vlad Tepes, better known as fiction's Count Dracula, held court here in the 15th century.**

Above: **The village of Sighisoara is famous for having a fortress that dates back to the 14th century.**

Opposite: **The village of Risnov in Transylvania.**

THE THREE PRINCIPALITIES

From the third to the 11th century, the Dacian region faced invasions of migratory peoples, including the Magyars and Slavs. The people in the region relied on the local voivode (VO-e-vod), or military leader, to protect them. In exchange, they gave their allegiance to him, paid tribute, and provided soldiers in times of danger. In 1330 several small voivodates in the south united under the leadership of Prince Basarab to establish the principality of Walachia. In 1359 the nobility in the east came together under the leadership of Prince Bogdan I. Their settlements were centered around the Moldova River.

Over time and a process of assimilation, the Romanian people as we know today were born. From the Middle Ages to the present, the Romanians lived in three neighboring principalities: Walachia, Moldavia, and Transylvania. The latter was part of the Hungarian kingdom from the 11th to 20th centuries. During this period, Walachia and Moldavia became religiously and culturally aligned to the Eastern Orthodox practices of the Byzantine Empire. They also based their written laws on the Byzantine codes. Occasional conflicts affected the stability of the principalities. In Transylvania the Romanian population was reduced to the status of serfs after a peasant rebellion in 1437 against the Magyar and Saxon nobles. The kingdoms of Hungary and Poland had designs on the principalities of Walachia and Moldavia, causing unrest among the nobility. The greatest threat of all, and the one that would prove most significant, came from the south, where the mighty Ottoman Empire was making its ascendance.

TRANSYLVANIA

There are two histories of Transylvania, the Romanian and the Hungarian versions. Hungarian scholars claim that between the ninth and 13th centuries, when the Magyars arrived and settled in Transylvania, the original inhabitants were Slavs, not Romanians. Romanian scholars, on the other hand, believe that Dacians and Romans intermarried and settled in Transylvania before the Magyars arrived. Whoever came first, they were joined by German settlers known as Saxons, who also stayed in the region. The ruling nobility was mainly made up of Europeans, including Magyars, who received the support of the Austrian Habsburg Empire, which involved the Kingdom of Hungary. Despite a revolt by Romanian peasants in 1784 and 1785, Hungarian influence was reinforced in the years that followed. During the 19th century, when nationalism was a potent force in Europe, the Kingdom of Hungary began a policy of Magyarization. It did so under the mantle of the Habsburg dynasty with the intention of strengthening Hungarian culture in the region. For instance, Hungarian was made the official language.

When Romania entered World War I in 1916, Hungarian forces in Transylvania were attacked. With the collapse of the Austro-Hungarian Empire after the war, Transylvania was united with Romania. During World War II, a part of Transylvania was given to Hungary by Hitler's Vienna Dictate. With the victory of the Allies, Transylvania was fully reunited with Romania in 1947. Since the fall of the anti-Hungarian Communist government, Romania and Hungary have taken steps to improve relations. Transylvania today is home to a Hungarian minority.

Michael the Brave, prince of Walachia (1593–1601), was the first leader to achieve political unity of the principalities of Walachia, Moldavia, and Transylvania.

TURKISH RULE

The 14th and 15th centuries were marked by the Romanians' struggle to withstand the spread of Ottoman rule, and though these struggles were intermittently successful, Ottoman power prevailed. Romanians identify many of their heroes from this period. Before Walachia succumbed, Vlad the Impaler (1448, 1456–62, 1476) led a defiant resistance, as did Alexander the Good of Moldavia (1401–31) and Stephen the Great (1457–1504). Stephen the Great defeated the Hungarians and Poles as well as the Turks. He is also famous for the monasteries and churches he built.

It was during the period of Ottoman rule that the three principalities of Walachia, Moldavia, and Transylvania were first united under Michael the Brave of Walachia. Michael's conquest of Transylvania in 1600 proved brief, and resistance to Turkish rule soon crumbled after he was assassinated in 1601. Other princes, who had no qualms about accepting the yoke of foreign domination, went down in Romanian history labeled with epithets like Basil the Locust, Ion the Cruel, and Aron the Tyrant.

After the death of Michael the Brave, the Turks reasserted their control and dispatched Greek officials to rule the region. The Greeks were known as the Phanariots because they came from the Phanar district of Constantinople, Turkey. Many of the Phanariot princes were corrupt, and their hold over the Romanians was never very strong. The Phanariots paid large bribes to the Ottomans in order to be established as princes, and they recouped this expenditure many times over by exploiting the native peasants. Between 1711 and 1821, more than 70 new princes were crowned in Walachia and Moldavia, and ordinary Romanians were reduced to their worst state ever. During the late 1700s, however, the Turks suffered military defeats at the hands of the Russian and Habsburg armies, and Turkey began to lose its influence.

A NATION EMERGES

As Ottoman power declined, Russia and the Habsburg monarchy squabbled for parts of the region. In 1821 there was a popular rebellion in Walachia against Phanariot rule, and the leader of the uprising, Tudor Vladimirescu, stirred nationalist emotions to a new pitch before he was executed.

The Greeks left after the Treaty of Adrianpole in 1829, only to be replaced by Russian rule and a new constitution. The new regime granted some autonomy to Romanian nobles in return for supporting Russia and not Austria. By 1834 the region was sufficiently stable for Russian troops to withdraw.

The idea of uniting Walachia and Moldavia had been developing throughout the period of Turkish rule, and the time was now ripe for its realization. In 1859 Prince Alexandru Ioan Cuza was elected as head of Walachia and Moldavia. In 1866 these principalities became collectively known as Romania, or Rumania, as it was then spelled. A new ruler, Prince Carol, a German prince, also emerged in 1866. Eleven years into his rule, he led a combined Romanian and Russian army that defeated the Turks at the Battle of Plevna. At the Congress of Berlin in 1879, Turkish rule officially came to an end. Soon after, in 1881, Prince Carol became King Carol I, the first king of Romania.

Alexandru Ioan Cuza (1859–66) was the first prince to unite the principalities of Moldavia and Walachia.

Proclamation of the new Romanian Constitution being posted in the streets of Bucharest in February 1938.

A PERIOD OF UNREST

Between independence and the outbreak of World War II, Romania underwent dramatic developments. After centuries of foreign rule, Romanians finally had their own constitution. But for the peasants who made up the majority of the population, life remained harsh. A feudal system still existed in Romania, and the large landowners, despite their small numbers, wielded much political power. The peasants' plight was ignored by the nobility-led Romanian government, which was more anxious to make deals with Western European capitalists interested in exploiting Romania's natural resources. In 1907 a rural uprising occurred, and rich estates were attacked and burned. The army crushed the rebellion, killing 10,000 peasants, and an uneasy peace was restored.

In 1914, when World War I erupted, Ferdinand I succeeded Carol I. The Trianon Treaty doubled the size of Romania by its union with Transylvania, Bucovina (now in southern Ukraine), and Bessarabia (now the Republic of Moldova). Unfortunately, land reforms undertaken after World War I did not improve the lives of peasants. Social unrest developed, made worse by imperialist threats from Communist Russia, the rise of fascist movements in Europe, and the Great Depression of 1929–33. Massive unemployment encouraged support for the fascists, who blamed non-ethnic Romanians and the Communists for the country's ills.

Carol II was crowned king in 1930, but the new regime failed to tackle the country's social and economic problems. The army was used to crush industrial unrest, and in 1938 the king banned all political parties. The leader of the fascist Iron Guard movement was executed. Romania was a deeply divided country when World War II broke out in 1939.

WORLD WAR II

Fearing a Russian invasion of Romania's northeastern territories, Carol II negotiated with Hitler in 1939 and 1940. He was forced to abdicate after substantial parts of Romania were taken by Hungary and Russia. His son Michael became king, but power was in the hands of General Ion Antonescu. Antonescu, who was believed to be anti-Semitic, supported Germany, whom he hoped would help Romania recover Bessarabia and Bucovina, territories annexed by the Soviet Union in 1940. Romania joined Germany in the invasion of Russia in 1941, where the Axis forces suffered heavy losses.

A demonstration held in Bucharest by the Iron Guard in December 1940. Support for this fascist movement in Romania increased with Hitler's rise to power in 1933, even though the Iron Guard did not have official ties with the Nazis. Marshal Antonescu abolished the movement in 1941.

While Antonescu initially permitted some Jews to emigrate, pogroms were also organized within Romania where thousands of Jews were executed. Jews in the newly recovered territories of Bessarabia and Bucovina were either killed or sent to camps in parts of Ukraine held by the Axis forces. By 1944 opposition to Nazism was increasing in Romania. King Michael overthrew Antonescu in August 1944, just as Russian troops crossed the border and occupied Romania.

Consequently, there was a powerful Soviet influence in the government of Romania after the end of the war in 1945. Most of Romania's confiscated land was returned after World War II, and there was a significant change in land reform policy that affected millions of peasants. Women were given the right to vote in 1946. King Michael was forced by the Soviet authorities to abdicate in 1947. Romania was declared a People's Republic, and Petru Groza headed the puppet Communist government.

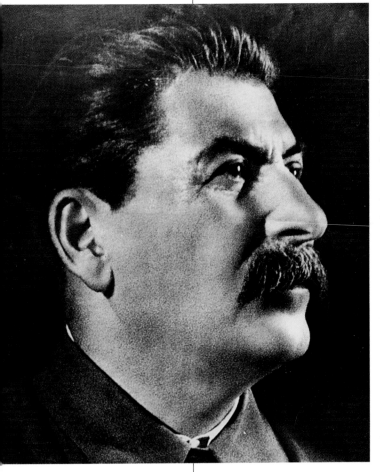

THE YEARS OF COMMUNISM

After 1947 Romania became a satellite state of what was then called the Soviet Union, a Russian-dominated union of Communist states opposed to the United States and Western Europe. The government, the economy, and the educational system were drastically reworked to resemble the system in the Soviet Union. Stalinist principles—so called after the leader of the Soviet Union at the time, Joseph Stalin—were introduced in Romania and remained in place until the late 1980s.

All industries, commercial enterprises, and banks were nationalized and placed under the control of the government. In the countryside, farmland was collectivized against the wishes of the majority of peasants, resulting in protests and the arrest of thousands. Collectivization meant that farmers no longer owned the land they worked, and small farms were forced to combine into large collectives under the control and management of the government.

Any person or organization that was unwilling to support the Communist regime, which was headed by Nicolae Ceausescu beginning in 1965, risked being punished. For instance, churches, especially those belonging to ethnic minorities that refused to cooperate with government policies, were disbanded. Political prisoners spent their time in jail or were sent to work on labor projects, such as the Danube-Black Sea canal, where the work was so dangerous it became known as the Canal of Death. The project claimed the lives of over 100,000 workers.

Romania did occasionally express its sense of independence by opposing the policies of the Soviet Union. Romania's Communist Party refused to support the Soviet Union's invasion of Czechoslovakia in 1968 and that of Afghanistan in 1981. A more symbolic gesture of independence was the country's decision to send a national team to the 1984 Los Angeles Olympics, defying the Soviet Union's boycott of the Games.

POPULAR REVOLUTION

In December 1989, thousands of people gathered in the city of Timisoara to protest the worsening of food shortages and to call for a relaxation of the controls exercised by the Ceausescu regime. There had been earlier protests in 1987, but those were stifled by a combination of police repression and a speedy supply of extra food to dissatisfied regions. This time Ceausescu chose to rely entirely on his security forces and ordered them to fire on demonstrators. Hundreds of protesters died. As news of this spread across the country, other protests spontaneously erupted. In Bucharest, security troops again fired on unarmed crowds. As the death toll went up, the mass protests continued. When some army units refused to carry out government orders, the protests turned into a popular revolution.

As citizens and the army fought with security forces, Ceausescu and his wife, Elena, fled from the capital but were soon captured by the army. After a hurried trial conducted by a military tribunal, they were found guilty of murder and executed by a firing squad.

Opposite: **Russian dictator Joseph Stalin (1879–1953) annexed parts of Romania and other countries of Eastern Europe during World War II. After the war, he continued to impose control on these countries.**

SHOEMAKER TO TYRANT

Nicolae Ceausescu and his wife, Elena, were executed on Christmas Day, 1989. The event was marked by a celebratory spirit across the country, a reaction that many outsiders found difficult to understand until details of Ceausescu's regime of terror came to be general knowledge.

Ceausescu came from a poor family, and after a very elementary education he began an apprenticeship as a shoemaker. He became interested in politics and rose quickly through the ranks of the Communist Party to become its general secretary in 1965. He became Romania's president two years later. As leader of the country, Ceausescu made many political maneuvers to ensure that he stayed in power. He appointed members of his family, notably his wife, to fill key leadership positions. He also gave the impression of being in opposition to Soviet authority by meeting with many Western leaders, including U.S. president Richard Nixon, who visited Romania in 1969 (*below*).

Behind the glamor, however, Ceausescu presided over a dreadful tyranny. Foreign books and movies were banned, and even typewriters had to be registered with the police. Individuals buying paper were likely to be interrogated by the state security police, the Securitate (SAE-ku-ri-TA-teh). The Securitate also enforced restrictions such as limiting families to only one 40-watt bulb per apartment. In 1981 Romanians were subject to bread rationing, and measures were taken to limit the consumption of basic foodstuffs, such as sugar, coffee, and flour, while food was exported in an effort to pay off Romania's large foreign debt. Ceausescu's heavy-handed debt-reduction policies resulted in massive shortages of food, fuel, and medicines in the country. While most of the population suffered terrible hardship during this time, the Ceausescus lived luxuriously.

FREE ELECTIONS

After the revolution, the Council of the National Salvation Front (FSN), with Ion Iliescu (Yon E-li-ES-ku) as its chairman, took over. Free elections were held for the first time in 1990. But the people's wishes for a government clean of ex-Communists were not fulfilled. The FSN, now a political party, won a landslide victory despite common knowledge that the newly elected president, Ion Iliescu, and most members of the FSN government had worked for Ceausescu and were members of the Communist Party.

While Romanians voted for change, they did so cautiously. There was no overwhelming desire to vote for a totally new system overnight. Discontent against the provisional government, directed mainly at Ion Iliescu, soon developed. In June 1990, thousands of coal miners were summoned to crush protesters who were demonstrating against the FSN government in Bucharest. At the time, coal miners were loyal supporters of the FSN. A year later, in September 1991, the coal miners, by this time disillusioned with the government, demonstrated against the FSN.

Ion Iliescu was reelected in the 1992 presidential elections. But by 1996, inflation had risen sharply, the economy had stagnated, and corruption was rife. Romanians showed their unhappiness by electing Emil Constantinescu as their new president. An alliance of political parties formed the new government, but internal problems caused the economy to slow further. Rising nationalism also raised fears among minorities that they would again be oppressed. Thus in the 2000 presidential elections, Ion Iliescu, now with a new political party, was voted in again as president.

In March 2004 Romania became a part of the North Atlantic Treaty Organization (NATO) and is expected to be a member of the European Union (EU) in 2007. Romania hopes its entry into these organizations will bring about greater democracy and economic prosperity.

GOVERNMENT

FIVE MONTHS AFTER the December 1989 revolution, elections were held and a parliament was formed to draw up a new constitution for the country. Romania's last democratic constitution had been drawn up in 1923, but from 1947 until 1989, the country had been governed by communist leaders.

Romania's first post-Communist constitution came into force on December 8, 1991. It was revised in October 2003 to meet stringent European Union entry standards. Minorities in Romania hope that EU membership will bring greater tolerance of ethnic diversity.

Left: **Adopted in 1992, Romania's coat of arms consists of an eagle holding a cross in its beak, with a sword and a scepter in each claw. Also represented on the coat of arms are the symbols of some of Romania's provinces—Walachia, Moldavia, Transylvania, Banat, and Dobrogea.**

Opposite: **The massive Palace of Parliament in Bucharest. It is still called locally by its Communist-era name, House of the People.**

The Bucharest Press House in Press Square, from which all media was controlled during the Ceausescu regime.

THE WAY THINGS WERE

Between the end of World War II and the 1989 revolution, the dominant and controlling force in Romanian society was the Communist Party. What this meant was that the party leadership, headed by the general secretary, decided on all important matters of government. The party exercised the executive, or decision-making, powers of the state. There was an elected body of representatives, or legislature, that passed proposed new laws, but there was never any genuine debate. The legislature functioned like a rubber stamp, merely endorsing what had already been decided by the party.

Under the party dictatorship, the judicial process also lacked independence. The courts did not have the power to interpret and question the laws of the state. Instead, they only implemented the decisions made by the executive powers.

Before the new constitution of 1991, trade unions were controlled by the government and the right to strike was not recognized by law. Human rights took second place to the needs of the government, and there was a wide-ranging internal security system that interfered with the private lives of citizens. The government security police, the Securitate, had the power to arrest and imprison people arbitrarily.

THE TIMISOARA PROCLAMATION

A public gathering of over 15,000 people in Opera Square in the town of Timisoara on March 11, 1990, became a symbol of Romania's resolution to dissociate itself completely from the system of government that had existed for the previous 45 years. A proclamation was issued that began by declaring the Romanian revolution to be one strand of a broader movement across Eastern Europe that rejected the Communist system totally: "In keeping with the aspirations of millions of people in Eastern Europe, we demand the immediate abolition of this totalitarian and bankrupt system. The ideal of the revolution was and remains a return to the genuine values of democracy and European civilization."

The proclamation also insisted that former members of the Securitate be forbidden from running for parliament, and that those who had served the Communist regime should not be allowed to run for president in the new government. A few months later, when it was clear that this rule was being broken, thousands of demonstrators supporting the Timisoara Proclamation blocked University Square in Bucharest and a sit-in was organized. The acting government of the FSN responded by calling in coal miners to disband the protesters.

A NEW START

The provisional leaders of the government that emerged after the 1989 revolution called themselves the National Salvation Front (FSN). They quickly instituted measures designed to distance themselves from the former government. Shops were supplied with food that had been earmarked for export. Precious imported items like coffee and chocolate, which had been previously reserved for high-ranking party members, were suddenly available to the public, too. In addition, after the execution of Ceausescu, the death penalty was abolished. Many political prisoners were also released.

Free elections were announced for May 1990, but fears increased when the FSN, which originally claimed only to exist in order to help organize the transition to full democracy, decided to become a party of its own and contest the elections. During this time, about 200 political parties were formed, some of which emerged to challenge the FSN, since the FSN was mostly composed of former Communist Party members. However the FSN, under the leadership of Ion Iliescu, won most of the votes in the 1990 elections, and Iliescu became the country's president.

THE PRESIDENT OF ROMANIA

The office of president was first introduced in 1974 by Nicolae Ceausescu as a way of consolidating his own power. When the new constitution was being drawn up, there was heated debate over the issue of retaining a president or choosing a form of government known as a constitutional monarchy. The latter was the system that operated in Romania until 1947, and it could have been reintroduced as part of a democratically elected parliamentary system.

In 1990 the Romanian parliament voted to adopt a form of republican government with a president elected by universal suffrage. In 2003 the term of office for the president was changed from four to five years, and no one is allowed to hold the position of president for more than two terms. The last presidential elections were held in November 2004, but there was no clear winner. A run-off was held in December. Mayor of Bucharest Traian Basescu of the opposition centrist Justice and Truth Alliance won the run-off with around 52 percent of the votes to become Romania's new president.

The president's powers are clearly defined in the areas of national defense, security, and foreign affairs. The president is the supreme commander of the armed forces, and the chairperson of the Supreme Defense Council, and plays a major role in representing Romania abroad. The president also promulgates the laws passed by the parliament, and takes action during domestic and international crises.

THE 1991 CONSTITUTION

Romania is a republic with a democratically elected bicameral parliament and an elected president. The government consists of three main branches: legislative, executive, and judicial.

Under the 1991 constitution, Romania is "a sovereign, independent, unitary, and indivisible National State." All citizens are deemed equal, "without any discrimination on account of race, nationality, ethnic origin, language, religion, sex, opinion, political adherence, property, or social origin." The constitution especially heeds the rights and liberties of individuals because it was drawn up after a legacy of over 40 years of dictatorship. It is similar to the constitution of the United States in that it greatly emphasizes individual freedom.

A referendum in 2003 saw a major revision to bring the constitution in line with EU regulations. It included strengthening parliament's control over government; restricting parliamentarian immunity; stating more clearly minority rights; recognizing the multiparty political system as a condition of democracy; and guaranteeing the protection of private property from nationalization and other forms of forced transfer.

Ion Iliescu greets the crowd after he won Romania's first post-Communist presidential elections in 1990. Although he lost the next election held in 1996, he returned to power in 2000. In 2004, after serving his second term in office, Iliescu, as required by the constitution, stepped down as president.

THE PARLIAMENT

Romania's parliament is divided into the Senate, or the upper house, and the Chamber of Deputies, or the lower house. The parliament is the sole law making authority, and members of the parliament are elected by the people. The Romanian parliament consists of 345 deputies and 143 senators. Deputies and senators serve four-year terms. Romania's system of government is similar to the French system of government. In addition to the post of president, it also has a prime minister who heads the government. The president appoints the prime minister who, in turn, chooses the cabinet. The president can also dissolve parliament if it fails to approve a government within 60 days.

In 2000 Ion Iliescu was reelected as president and appointed Adrian Nastase to serve as prime minister. In end-2004, having served the maximum two terms in office, Iliescu stepped down as president. Nastase then ran for presidency in the 2004 elections, which he lost to Traian Basescu of the Justice and Truth Alliance. At the parliamentary elections held concurrently with the presidential elections, the Social Democrats were returned to power by a slim margin over the Justice and Truth Alliance, leaving neither party with enough seats to form a majority.

LOCAL GOVERNMENT

Romania is divided into 41 counties, or *judete* (joo-DEH-TSE), and one municipality—Bucharest. Each county is further subdivided into towns and communes and is led by a prefect, who is appointed by the government. The prefect represents the central government at a local level. County administration is autonomous and is governed by elected county councils, who coordinate the activities of the communes and town councils in their area. Town councils and mayors are elected by the people.

THE JUDICIARY

Romania's judiciary consists of the law courts, the Ministry of Justice, and the Superior Council of Magistrates. The law courts consist of the Supreme Court, the county courts and other lower courts, as well as the military tribunals. Judges of the Supreme Court are appointed by the president to serve a six-year term. Members of the Superior Council of Magistrates are elected by the parliament to serve four-year terms and recommend potential members of the Supreme Court to the president. The council also acts as a disciplinary court for the legal profession. The Constitutional Court was created to ensure that there is a balance of power among the various agencies within the government and that the laws passed are in line with the constitution. There are nine judges serving in the Constitutional Court. These judges serve nine-year terms and are appointed by the parliament and the president. The Ministry of Justice consists of prosecutors who represent the general interests of society, protecting rights and freedoms and maintaining order under the law. Public prosecutors are nominated by the Superior Council of Magistrates.

Above: **Two Romanian children cast the ballots for their parents at the local elections for mayors and councillors in 2000.**

Opposite: **Romania's parliament in session.**

ECONOMY

ROMANIA'S ECONOMY IS undergoing momentous and far-reaching changes. What was once a centralized economy controlled and dictated by the Communist Party is now going through a process of change into a free market economy. Romania is working together with the International Monetary Fund (IMF) and other international donors to strengthen its economy and align it to European Union standards in preparation for its membership in the EU in 2007. In the past few years, Romania has been successful in curbing inflation and reducing its foreign debt.

Cottage industries, particularly pottery, embroidery, and weaving, are found throughout Romania. But in some areas, traditional methods (*opposite*) have been replaced by machines such as this mechanized loom being worked by nuns (*below*).

Construction of the canal between Bucharest and Black Sea was initiated in the early 1970s, but work was abandoned due to insufficient financial resources.

LEGACY OF THE PAST

The enormous economic challenges facing Romania can only be appreciated by understanding the numerous problems inherited from the Ceausescu era.

The central government in Bucharest used to set production targets for various industries without regard for the country's raw materials or resources. Large sums of money were wasted in investment schemes whose motives were for political prestige rather than economic gain or profit. For example, Ceausescu ordered the building of a canal linking Bucharest with the Danube in order to bring prestige and wealth to the capital. It was an ambitious undertaking, especially in view of the country's limited resources at that time. Meanwhile, some industries that needed an injection of capital, such as the metallurgical and chemical industries, were forced to survive with outdated equipment.

Underlying these problems was the mounting foreign debt, a result of the massive loans required for the country's industrialization program. By 1981 the total debt was over $10 billion. The International Monetary Fund, the main financier, made difficult demands in return for rescheduling payments. Imports were severely reduced, especially of food, while meat continued to be exported in order to gain valuable foreign currency. This led to the rationing of meat in Romania.

In 1982 Ceausescu declared that the entire foreign debt would be paid off by 1990, and severe measures were introduced to save money. For example, bread, flour, sugar, milk, and gasoline were all rationed, with portions progressively reduced.

There was little money for purchasing new technologies, especially in the production of energy. The system for supplying gas and electricity across the country was never allowed to develop in proportion to the increase in demand. As a result, drastic measures, such as an 80 percent cut in street lighting in Bucharest from 1972 to 1989, were adopted. The law forbade office temperatures to exceed 57°F (13.8°C) when it was below zero outside. Hot water was only available once a week. During the bitter winter of 1984, medical records show that over 30 infants died in Bucharest's hospitals, the result of unannounced power cuts that affected their incubators.

Factory workers assembling tractor parts. Tractors are a major Romanian export.

ECONOMIC HISTORY

After World War II, Romania's leaders set about rapidly industrializing the country. The motive behind the drive to industrialize was as much political as economic. The Soviet Union would have been happy to have Romania remain an agricultural country to supply the Russian industrial workers with food. But Romania's sense of independence would not allow the country to become merely a granary that fed the Soviet Union. There was also a desire to move away from dependency upon power centered in Moscow. The Soviet Union opposed Romania's industrialization and refused to provide the necessary financial aid. As a result, Ceausescu turned to the West for loans. This meant that the country amassed a huge foreign debt. The severity of the economic situation was made worse by a powerful earthquake in 1977, with equally disastrous floods in 1980 and 1981, that badly disrupted industrial production. Determined to pay off the huge debt quickly, Ceausescu embarked on a debt-reduction strategy that wreaked havoc on the Romanian economy and the country's people.

Since the fall of the Ceausescu regime, Romania has sought to built a Western-styled free market economy. Today, Romania is making economic progress, but widespread poverty still remains.

TAKING RISKS

Recent measures taken toward decentralization have subjected the economy to normal market forces. Numerous unprofitable industries, previously protected by the central government, have closed down, resulting in unemployment. This is a major point in the political debate of the country. Full employment was a feature of Communist rule. Those who oppose the call for a radical and swift change to a market economy are alarmed at the risk of massive and sustained unemployment. This risk is especially high for industrial workers because factories can be shut down overnight if they are not profitable.

To modernize the economy, Romania has had to rely on foreign investors to bring in the much-needed capital. The present government has been somewhat successful in convincing foreign firms to base their factories in Romania.

The Romanian government initiated a law providing unemployment benefits in 1991, and the economic downturn in the early 1990s led to the creation of an improved social insurance system in 1994.

Above: **A small retail shop in Bucharest. Although recent economic reforms are aimed at encouraging small businesses, the lack of capital and expertise and the low wages are obstacles to achieving a true market economy.**

Opposite: **The Brazi refinery near Ploiesti (Prahova County), one of the best-known Romanian oil fields. The area is one of the largest and most modern centers of the Romanian petrochemical industry.**

Coca-Cola built a soft drink infrastructure in Romania in just two years. It is now the market leader throughout central and eastern Europe, including Romania, where it is one of the country's largest foreign investors.

FOREIGN INVESTMENT

Foreign investors are being wooed by the Romanian government in an attempt to bring Romania's economy back to life. Not only is an attractive investment package offered, but Romania's cheap, skilled labor force and advantageous geographic position (being close to the Russian Federation and the Middle East as well as having one of the largest markets in Central and Eastern Europe) make it highly attractive to foreign investors.

The range of incentives include noninterference by the government—foreign investments are secure from nationalization, expropriation, requisition, or other similar measures; 100 percent private ownership; deferral in tax payments if the company's investment is vital to Romania's economy; customs and value-added tax exemption on certain imports and acquisitions from overseas; customs and value-added tax exemptions on acquisition on the domestic market of raw materials, spare parts and components, and other specific items; and free access to markets in all sectors and equal treatment with Romanian investors.

In 2002 the government created the Romanian Agency for Foreign Investment to attract foreign investors and to promote Romania as a place to do business. Some of the largest foreign investors in Romania today include Citibank, ABN-Amro, Shell, Daewoo, Renault, Siemens, Orange, Colgate-Palmolive, Proctor and Gamble, and Coca-Cola. Between 1991 and 2003, the total foreign investment amounted to about 90 billion Euros ($111 billion). The Netherlands is Romania's largest foreign investor, followed by France, Germany, the United States, and Austria.

Freight trains carrying cars made in Romania to the port of Constanta for export. Major car firms such as Volvo have entered into joint ventures with Romanian firms to manufacture and assemble automobiles and auto parts.

PRIVATIZATION

Before the 1989 revolution there were no privately owned factories or farms. They were all owned by the state. A process of privatization is now being implemented to convert state-owned businesses to private businesses.

In 1991 a law was passed that transferred, in the form of property certificates, 30 percent of the registered capital of state-owned commercial companies, free of charge, to Romanian citizens. The remaining 70 percent of businesses under state ownership were to be sold to private individuals, or companies, including foreign investors.

Romanian banks have also since been privatized. Private enterprise is also returning to the once largely state-owned industrial sector. The Romanian Development Agency was set up to encourage the growth of small-to-medium enterprises. State farms have also been broken up and returned to the families that once owned and farmed them. More than 80 percent of Romania's arable land is now under private ownership.

ENERGY RESOURCES

Romania has large coal and oil deposits, including oil fields discovered in its section of the Black Sea in 1981. The country is the largest oil producer in Central and Eastern Europe. Romania is also the largest producer of natural gas in Eastern Europe. Natural gases, such as methane, are found in the Transylvanian Plateau. Romania, however, still needs to import natural gas from Russia to meet all of its domestic power needs.

A nuclear power plant in Cernavoda, located on the lower Danube, accounts for about 10 percent of the country's electricity production. The Romanian government hopes to have a second reactor working by 2006 to increase Romania's power output. The country also relies on hydroelectric power plants to meet its energy needs. About 30 percent of Romania's power generation is hydroelectricity. The Romanian government plans to develop new nuclear and hydroelectric power facilities.

SOURCES OF EMPLOYMENT

In 1999 Romania's labor force numbered 10 million people. Despite the large number of working people, the unemployment rate is 7.3 percent. While the Romanian economy is improving, about 45 percent of people in Romania live below the poverty line.

INDUSTRY Due to the massive industrialization program between 1947 and 1970, industry is a major source of employment. Steelworks, metallurgical complexes, machine-building, and metal-processing all involve large-scale factories. The industrial sector employs about 27 percent of Romania's labor force and provides 35 percent of the country's gross domestic product (GDP).

A tremendous variety of products is made by factory workers, ranging from machine parts to diesel engines and tractors. Furniture, footwear, clothes, and textiles are also manufactured, and they compete favorably in the international market. Romania's metallurgical industry is another key industry and has a long history dating back to Roman times, when gold and silver were mined in the southwestern and western parts of the country. These metals, along with silver and aluminum, are still mined today. The metal-processing and machine-building industries account for almost one-third of the total industrial production.

FORESTRY Forests cover nearly 27 percent of Romania, giving rise to a thriving lumber industry. Hardwoods like oak and beech are used for making furniture and as building materials. Fir is used in the construction of boats and the manufacture of musical instruments.

AGRICULTURE Despite the intense process of industrialization, agriculture is still the main source of employment. Around 60 percent of the land is arable. The rich agricultural land of Romania, blessed with a suitable climate, encourages the development of cereal crops, such as wheat, corn, rye, and oats. The agricultural sector provides 15 percent of the GDP and employs about 40 percent of Romania's workforce. Wine production is one of the more thriving industries, and increasing amounts of wine are being exported. Romania is now one of the top 10 wine producers in Europe, and Romanian white and red wines have won international recognition.

Musical instruments made from Romanian wood supply the demands of the export market. Mures province is well known for its production of wooden musical instruments.

FISHING The rivers and lakes of Romania, and particularly the Danube delta area and the Black Sea coastal region, support a valuable fishing industry that supplies the local and export market. Caviar, the eggs of sturgeon fish, are also an important export. Domestic demand for fresh fish is high. The extra fish goes to processing factories for canning and export. Fishing is becoming an important source of revenue and employment.

ENVIRONMENT

NEARLY HALF OF ROMANIA is in a natural or seminatural state. With mountains, glaciers, wetlands, and flatlands, Romania is rich in animal and plant life. Some animal and plant species that are no longer found in other European countries can still be found in Romania. Today, however, growing economic development has placed pressure on Romania's fragile environment. In view of the country's pending membership in the European Union, Romania has adopted several environmental conservation laws. Many international organizations, such as the World Wildlife Fund (WWF) and the World Bank, have provided funds to help the Romanian government develop sound environmental management programs.

NATIONAL PARKS AND PROTECTED AREAS

Romania boasts nine national parks, six nature parks and three UNESCO biosphere reserves. The country has about 845 protected areas, which together make up more than 5 percent of the country's land area.

The country's first environmental protection law was passed in 1930. Over the next few years, several national parks and reserves were created, including the Retezat National Park in the Southern Carpathians and the Pietrosul Mare National Park in the Western Carpathians. The Ceahlau Massif National Park in the Eastern Carpathians has unique rock formations that have inspired many myths. The massif is said to be the home of Zamolxe, God of the Dacians, who were the ancestors of today's Romanian people.

In 1990 Romania's Danube delta, with its unique ecological system, was designated a UNESCO biosphere reserve. The delta is Europe's largest wetland area and has the largest reed bed in the world. It is home to a vast range of plants and animals. The Danube delta is also on the WWF's list of the top 200 most important areas for biodiversity.

Opposite: **The reed beds of the Danube delta are the most extensive in the world.**

The village of Sacele near the city of Brasov in the Transylvania region. The forest-covered slopes of the Carpathian Mountains loom in the background. Traditional methods of farming are less harmful on Romania's forests.

FORESTS AND FORESTRY

Romania's forests cover nearly 27 percent of the country and consist mainly of deciduous hardwood trees such as beech, sycamore, maple, ash, and elm. Much of Romania's forest cover has remained untouched. Because of the remoteness of the Carpathians, the Communist government did not bother to turn much of the forests into state-owned farms. At the same time, farming relied mainly on traditional methods using few chemical pesticides and fertilizers.

Two major factors are slowly changing the face of the Carpathians, especially in the lower foothills. Logging has been a major industry in Romania, and the country is one of the leading exporters of timber. This means that many trees are felled to supply the profitable timber industry. Illegal logging is also a problem. The World Bank estimates that 5 to 20 percent of all timber cutting in Romania is illegal. The second factor is land restitution, where state land is returned to the original private owners. In 1991 the Romanian government planned to return about 7.4 million acres

(3 million hectares), or about one-third of Romania's forests, to individuals and communities whose land was seized by the Communist government. According to studies, many forests have been cut down because of the absence of legislature preventing these owners from felling trees.

In 2004 the World Bank and the Romanian government launched the $34-million Forestry Development Project. The project aims to improve and ensure better management and use of both state and private forests.

The Carpathians are like the Alps and spread across seven European countries, including Romania. The Carpathians are home to the largest virgin forests in Europe. The area contains 60 percent of all of Europe's brown bear population and 40 percent of the continent's wolf and lynx populations.

ECOTOURISM

Ecotourism is a growing industry in Romania. International organizations and some local associations provide funds and advice to rural communities to help them start their own ecotours.

These funds also improve the infrastructure and management of sites visited by tourists. Mountain climbing, trekking through the country's mountains and forests, camping, exploring caves, and bird-watching (*right*) are some activities being encouraged. Visits to medieval castles, the home of "Dracula," hot springs, and farm stays also provide revenue without destroying Romania's natural landscape.

A wolf peers from behind its enclosure in the Carpathian mountains. It is part of a conservation effort to ensure the survival of the animal in Romania.

SURVIVAL OF THE RARE

Many of Europe's most endangered and vulnerable animals live in Romania's virgin forests and wetlands. The Romanian Carpathians are home to 6,000 brown bears, some 2,500 wolves, and 1,500 lynxes, or about 40 percent of Europe's lynx population.

The Danube delta is home to around 360 species of birds that include Europe's largest colonies of Dalmatian pelicans and white pelicans, as well as rare or near-extinct birds. The Danube and its tributaries teem with fish such as perch, pike, sturgeon, and carp. Occasionally, small groups of Black Sea dolphins can be spotted swimming along the coast and rivers.

The poaching of Romania's animals, however, is a concern. Black Sea dolphins are often caught and sold to aquariums. World demand for caviar has resulted in the illegal fishing of sturgeon from Romania's waterways.

Wolves are shot because of superstition and because they attack livestock. Chamois are poached for their valuable hide.

Educational programs and laws have been put in place to discourage many of these practices. But weak enforcement and lack of government funding, as well as air and water pollution, mean that Romania's natural environment is still under threat.

POLLUTION

The Danube and its tributaries have been seriously affected by toxic mine spills, industrial discharge, and the recent war in neighboring Serbia when bombed out chemical and fertilizer factories spilled their toxic brew into the rivers. The Danube and some of its tributaries flow into the Black Sea, bringing their pollutants with them.

Fish stocks in the Black Sea have been in decline for several years due to pollution. For instance, three of the six sturgeon species found in the Danube river basin are either extinct or very rare. Untreated or semitreated sewage discharge from homes and industrial wastewater along the coast are major problems. Agricultural pollutants that drain into the rivers end up polluting the Black Sea.

Air pollution in Romania is due mainly to industrial activity and urban traffic. The energy sector is a major contributor to the pollution because it relies heavily on the burning of fossil fuels. Poorer households burn low-quality coal for heat, adding to the problem. Old and poorly maintained vehicles that run on leaded gasoline contribute to the pollution.

Fortunately, the signs for the future are good. A decline in industrial activity, an increasing use of alternative power sources, and more stringent regulations have led to improvements in the quality of air over urban and industrial parts of Romania.

Environmental pollution is a major problem in Romania. It has existed since the Communist era, and especially during the years of the Ceausescu regime.

POISONING THE DANUBE

Europe's second longest river has suffered many accidents. In late January 2000 approximately 3.5 million cubic feet (100,000 cubic meters) of wastewater contaminated with cyanide spilled from a gold mine in the northwestern city of Baia Mare into several rivers. The Tisza River, Hungary's second largest river and a major tributary of the Danube, was the most seriously affected. Yugoslav and Hungarian officials reported finding hundreds of dead fish in the lower reaches of the river. Dead fish were also found in the Danube River. The Hungarian authorities cleared around 300 tons of dead fish from the Tisza River (*below*). Later that same year, in March, two accidents two weeks apart at the state-owned Borsa mine in the Maramures region saw toxic mine waste flowing into parts of the Tisza River that had escaped the first contamination. Concentrations of lead in the Tisza River were found to be double that of European Union safety levels. The three toxic spills killed wildlife and affected the water supply for river communities.

NATO bombings in 1999 in Yugoslavia also polluted the Danube and its tributaries. Chemical plants along the rivers were attacked and poisonous heavy metals spilled into the rivers. In each case, both human and animal populations along the Danube and its tributaries were adversely affected. People could not use the water from the rivers for several weeks for their daily needs. They had to rely on piped water. Fishermen lost their livelihood when the fish died. Waterfowl that relied on a fish diet declined in great numbers. Fish and other wildlife have slowly returned to the Danube and Tisza rivers, but it will take years before the long-term effects of such contamination are known.

ALTERNATIVE ENERGY

Romania relies on fossil fuels, nuclear power, and hydroelectric power to meet its domestic energy needs. To decrease the country's reliance on fossil fuels, alternative energy sources are attractive. Romania currently has one nuclear reactor, with a second nuclear reactor planned, and a few hydroelectric power plants. Romania also has 38 geothermal systems that use hot water rising up from deep below the ground to heat homes and for industrial and agricultural uses.

Geothermal energy systems are especially environmentally friendly as they produce very few unhealthy byproducts and take up less space than conventional power plants. Unfortunately, as with other environmentally friendly energy systems currently in use on a small scale, geothermal usage in Romania suffers from a lack of funds and interest.

A hydroelectric dam on the Danube River near the town of Orsova.

ROMANIANS

THE PEOPLE OF ROMANIA trace their origins to Roman times and this is reflected in the name of the country, which means Land of the Romans. There is, however, a significant number of Hungarians in the population, who live chiefly in the western part of the country in Transylvania. Roma, or gypsies, are found throughout Romania. The second most populous ethnic minority is the Germans, also known as Saxons or Swabians.

Some 20 other nationalities live in Romania, including Serbs, Turks, Bulgarians, Tatars, and Armenians, but their total number is only a tiny fraction of the 9 million Romanians who live outside the borders of their own country.

Left: **Two shepherds drink** *tuica* **(TSUI-kuh), or plum brandy, in a local bar.**

Opposite: **A Romanian family.**

THE ROMAN CONNECTION

The intermarriage of Dacians and the conquering Romans (made up of troops from Rome and other parts of the Roman Empire, such as Greece and Spain) is viewed by modern Romanians to be their ethnic foundation. The presence of Romans in the country must have continued well beyond the formal withdrawal of Roman troops in A.D. 271 and 275. Supporting evidence for this theory comes from the fact that the Romanian language—clearly Latinate in its structure—could not have evolved the way it did if the Romans completely evacuated the land in the third century. Archeological evidence of coins bearing Roman inscriptions up to the fifth century has also been found. This suggests that commercial links between the Dacians and the Roman Empire continued after Roman troops withdrew.

THE QUESTION OF TRANSYLVANIA

Transylvania is historically important to both Romania and Hungary, and the issue of ownership has caused conflict between the two countries. Hungarians claim that the Magyars (Hungarians) came to Transylvania in the ninth century and are the rightful inhabitants of the land. Romanians claim that the region was already populated by the Romanized Dacians and that there were already ethnic Romanian principalities there when the Magyars arrived and conquered the region. The Romanian historical account also points out that when Austro-Hungary was formed in 1867 and Transylvania was incorporated into Hungary, the Hungarian government had a policy of forced Magyarization of the Romanian population. In 1918 Transylvania officially became part of Romania. This was confirmed by the 1920 Trianon Treaty that finalized the break-up of the Austro-Hungarian Empire. The northern part of Transylvania was given to Hungary in 1940, but was subsequently restored to Romania in 1947.

Above: **Two sides of a Roman coin. A portrait of Emperor Honorius (A.D. 395–423) is shown on one side, and the symbol for Constantinople is on the other. Such coins remained a medium of exchange in Romania until the 11th century.**

Opposite: **A street market in Brasov, Transylvania.**

56

The Hungarian name for Transylvania is Erdély (ER-day). Some Hungarians accuse the Romanian government of a campaign of ethnic cleansing to suppress the separate identity of the Hungarian minority in Transylvania. For example, Hungarian-language schools were closed down, and history books were written to correspond with the Romanian account of Transylvania's history.

Since 1989, the Romanian and Hungarian governments have worked to improve their strained relations, which began during the Communist era. In 1996 Romania and Hungary signed a treaty of understanding, cooperation, and good-neighborliness. The treaty, known as the Basic Treaty, was signed at Timisoara. Hungarian-language schools have also reopened in Transylvania.

Conflicts involving Hungarians living in Transylvania are particularly significant because Romania's ethnic Hungarians form the largest minority group in Romania and are nearly 21 percent of Transylvania's population. Despite the government's promises, restitution of property and other rights to ethnic Hungarians

have been slow. To ensure their views are represented in parliament, ethnic Hungarians formed their own political party, UDMR, in 1989, advocating territorial political autonomy. The UDMR has been a member of the ruling coalition since 1996.

Roma women in Sibiu, Transylvania. Owing to the migratory nature of the Roma, their absence in official census returns and their classification with other nomadic groups makes it difficult to estimate the total number of Roma in Romania. Few Roma are nomadic today because many were settled during the Communist era.

THE ROMA MINORITY

The Roma were a migratory people who came from northern India and settled in Europe in the 14th century. Some of the Roma in Romania are believed to have been brought as slaves by Ottoman rulers. When slavery was abolished, the Roma were given Romanian citizenship. Roma have their own language, Romany, which is thought to derive from Sanskrit. Roma in Romania often speak a combination of Romany and Romanian or Hungarian.

Romania has about 500,000 Roma, but many believe that there are almost 1.2 million Roma living in Romania. This is because some Roma do not want to be identified as Roma because of the prejudice they face. Roma are generally ostracized by Romanian society. In a 2003 Gallup poll, 31 percent of Romanians thought that Roma should not be allowed in public places such as restaurants and bars.

Roma traditionally tend to live in makeshift dwellings or shantytowns on the outskirts of big cities, especially around Bucharest, because they were not allowed to live in the cities. Today, Roma still live in poverty, and many of their homes lack basic facilities, such as electricity and water. Many Roma are either unemployed or employed in low-paying jobs, because the prejudice against them makes it difficult to obtain work. The Romanian government has taken steps to provide Roma with more opportunities to promote their culture and language. Poverty and social discrimination, however, remain the two main problems for the Roma, and they still face violence and harassment.

• Some 89 percent of Romania's 22.3 million people are Romanians.
• There are about 1.6 million Hungarians, making up about 6.6 percent of the population.
• Over 500,000 Roma make up 2.5 percent of the population. The real figure is estimated at 1.2 million as many Roma do not have fixed homes and may declare themselves as Hungarians or Romanians in the national census.
• There are about 60,000 Germans left in Romania, making up about 0.3 percent of Romania's population.

• Other nationalities include Ukrainians and Russians, constituting 0.3 percent and 0.2 percent of the population respectively. Turks make up 0.2 percent of the population. There are also small numbers of Serbians, Tatars, Slovakians, Bulgarians, Jews, Croats, Greeks, and Armenians. Together they make up about 4 percent of the country's population.

DISAPPEARING MINORITIES

Germans, mainly Saxons, were not granted the unrestricted right to leave Romania during the Ceausescu era. The German government campaigned for their right to leave and criticized the Romanian government's practice of granting exit permits in return for cash payments. Since the reunification of Germany and the 1989 revolution, there has been an outflow of Germans from Romania. Also in return for cash payments, the Ceausescu regime allowed Romanian Jews to leave for Israel. Before World War II, Romania was home to the third largest community of Jews in Eastern Europe, after Poland and the Soviet Union. However, emigration, deportation, and the extermination pogroms carried out in Bucharest, Iasi and other cities changed this. It is estimated that between 250,000 and 300,000 Romanian Jews were killed during the Romanian Holocaust. Today, about 9,000 to 15,000 Jews live in Romania, most of them in Bucharest.

TRADITIONAL COSTUME

Peasant women have traditionally made clothing by spinning, weaving, and sewing material made from wool, flax, cotton, and rough silk. The colorful embroidery work characteristic of traditional Romanian costume has also been associated with women. Men have tended to specialize in the making of vests, jackets, coats, and other garments made from leather or sheepskin.

Basic to a woman's costume is the simple white blouse embroidered with colorful ornamentation in bright red, black, and gold. A skirt is worn over the blouse and an apron is tied at the waist with a sash. The aprons and skirts tend to feature geometric patterns woven into or embroidered on them. Scarves and veils are worn, with a long thin silk veil being reserved for special occasions. Colored headgear is popular, and regional traditions have evolved their own ways of denoting a married woman by the kind of headdress she wears.

Romanians in their elaborate and beautifully embroidered traditional dress. Because of regional differences, Romania has a variety of national costumes.

The white blouse is also a basic item in male costume, tightened at the waist with a woolen sash or leather belt. This is usually worn with narrow, white trousers. A typical piece of headgear for men is the hat made of lambskin, black felt, or straw—depending on the time of year and the local tradition.

Over the centuries, traditional costume accommodated new materials and fashions. Today, Romanians dress in a similar fashion to North Americans; but for special occasions and in less developed, rural parts of the country, traditional costume is still worn and highly regarded.

ORDINARY ROMANIANS

The typical citizen has a sense of pride in being a Romanian. In a country surrounded by more than a dozen different nationalities and races, mostly Slavic and non-Latin, Romanians take pride in their Dacian roots and long history. Pride also exists in the fact that their country has preserved its own language and religion in spite of repeated assaults on its culture by the Austro-Hungarian and Ottoman empires, and more recently by the former Soviet Union.

Romanians, especially rural Romanians, are said to be hospitable, resourceful, good-natured, and often self-critical. The simple architecture of some small rural churches and country homes, reflecting an old-fashioned modesty, is now gradually replaced by ambitious, massive, and monumental buildings, for example, some Eastern Orthodox churches.

During the 1970s and 1980s, ordinary people were brutalized by the constant struggle to survive and became progressively demoralized. Having been watched constantly by the state police for decades, many observers agree that it will take a long time for Romanians to shrug off the sense of suspicion and intense self-interest that was imposed on the otherwise warm Romanian personality. Nevertheless, it is astonishing how, in spite of having endured such harsh conditions, a sense of goodwill is preserved, especially in rural areas where the tradition of welcoming a guest is still strong.

A birthday celebration with the extended family. Romanians in rural areas tend to have larger families than those living in urban areas.

Costume from Fagaras, Transylvania

Costume of Muscel in Walachia

Costume from Suceava, Moldavia

Costume from Hunedoara, Banat

COSTUMES OF ROMANIA

Traditional dress in Romania varies greatly from one region to another. But there are some common features.

For example, all men wear a cap or hat with their traditional costume, and the long white shirt is essential for both men and women's costumes.

The women's vests have rich embroidery. The regional differences are mainly in the colors used, the patterns of embroidery, and the accessories worn.

The skirts, also rich with decorative patterns, are usually made of woolen fabric. Footwear, such as sandals, moccasins, or boots are made of leather.

Costume from Dolj in Walachia

Costume from Hateg, Translyvania

Costume from Gorj, Walachia

The Saxon (German) costume

Costume of the Maramures region

Costume of ethnic Hungarians

Costume from Valea Argesului, Transylvania

ROMANIANS: A STUDY IN CONTRASTS

The one Romanian who is known throughout the West as Count Dracula is the least worthy representative of his country. Indeed, there could be no more dramatic contrast than one between the semifictional Dracula and the ordinary Romanian. What complicates the matter is that the historical character behind the Dracula story is a highly respected figure in Romanian history, famous for his successful war against the Turks and esteemed as a fighter for national independence.

DRACULA—AN EXTRAORDINARY ROMANIAN

The novel *Dracula*, written by the Irish writer Bram Stoker in 1898, helped turn Vlad Tepes into a legend that later caught the eye of Hollywood film producers. Stoker had studied accounts of vampirism in Europe, delved into Romanian folklore that included a belief in vampirism, and read about

Vlad the Impaler. He combined elements of all three, and *Dracula* was the result.

The man behind the legend was a Walachian prince known as Vlad the Impaler (1431–76). His father had been a king of Walachia, and had fought against the Ottoman army. As a reward for his illustrious service, he was knighted into the Order of Dracul. Dracul comes from the Latin word *dracu* (DRA-ku), meaning for snake or dragon.

When Vlad the Impaler became ruler of Walachia in 1456, he established a fearsome reputation for his method of punishment: spreadeagling bound victims, raising them off the ground on the end of stakes, and leaving them aloft to die in prolonged and awful pain. Other such punishments included boiling a captive alive.

Vlad the Impaler's dreadful reputation spread. At home, his brutal manner of punishing criminals produced a subdued and frightened populace. There is an account of how he left a golden cup by an isolated fountain for continued public use as he was confident that no one would dare steal it.

Vlad the Impaler became a national hero by his defiance of the Ottoman Turks. In 1462, Vlad successfully attacked their camp one night and, so the story goes, had 20,000 Turkish captives impaled on a forest of stakes. The Turks, demoralized and horrified, withdrew immediately. Vlad the Impaler was killed in 1476 while fighting the Turks in Bucharest.

Above: **Vlad Tepes, prince of Walachia. This photo was taken from an original painting in Castle Ambras in Tyrol.**

Opposite: **Romanian girls at a school.**

65

LIFESTYLE

THE LEGACY OF Ceausescu's bitter dictatorship continues to be felt decades after his fall. Romanians found the first decade of democracy a difficult period as they tried to cope with market forces and the removal of subsidies. They had thought their lives would improve immediately and were disappointed to discover that their standard of living had worsened instead.

Where lines for bread and meat used to snake around city blocks and empty shelves were once a common sight in stores, today lines are for fast food counters and good privately-baked bread. Shelves are filled with produce and meat. A few supermarkets have sprouted up in Bucharest that stock imported items. Computer ownership is also increasing. Such luxuries, however, are still restricted to the wealthier classes. The price of cars and television sets are exorbitant for most of the country's people. Internet use, while increasing, is still lower than in most European cities. Many Romanians cannot afford good healthcare, and hospitals are poorly funded. The life expectancy of Romanians is still much lower than that of their counterparts in Western Europe.

In 2004 Bucharest was rated the cheapest European city to live in, but it is certainly not cheap for most of its citizens. Increasing inflation in the transitional period after 1989 led observers to believe Romania had become a victim of economic forces. Subsequent governments have managed to control and bring down inflation, lessening fears of an economic disaster. Still, inflation hovers above 10 percent, and nearly half of the country's population live below the poverty line. The Romanians, however, are a resilient people who will not let adversity put them down.

Above: **Romanians in Bucharest line up in the winter cold outside a private bakery to buy bread, which costs twice as much as bread sold in state shops.**

Opposite: **An old man from Barsana village in the Maramures region. Privatization of land after 1989 has created a new social revolution in Romania's countryside.**

Romanian woman living in an old age home in lasi.

FROM BLACK TO WHITE

Life during the Communist period in the small town of Copsa Mica (COP-sha MI-ke) in Transylvania was once difficult and dangerous.

The town was notorious for its industrial pollution, although it was not unique in this respect. The pollution came from the town's two factories where smokestacks expelled thousands of tons of black dust into the sky. The pollution poisoned the land, and plants would not grow.

Half the town suffered from bronchitis or asthma, and two out of every three children had some form of mental retardation. The life expectancy was also nine years below the national average and the infant mortality rate was high.

In the 1990s the United Nations worked alongside the Romanian government to improve matters. The factory that produced black carbon for tires was shut down. The metalworks factory employed half the people in the town. It was not shut down but had special filters and disposal systems installed to keep the contaminants out of the air. A water treatment plant was built to prevent the factory from fouling nearby lakes and rivers.

Today, after seven years and at a cost of $250,000, Copsa Mica is now significantly cleaner. Gardens bloom where the land was once bare. Children can also play in the open without fear of blackening themselves or falling ill. Women can hang laundry outside without fear of the laundry becoming dirty again. Best of all, after 60 years of black, dirty snow, children can play with clean, white snow.

A DANGEROUS LIFE

Small towns like Copsa Mica (*right*) were an example of the dangers faced by ordinary working Romanians during Ceausescu's industrialization drive. Two plants were built in the town: a tyre factory and a metalworks factory. The pollution they produced gave Copsa Mica the unwanted label of being the most polluted city in Europe.

The tyre factory released pollutants into the air in the form of black dust that settled over everything and caused respiratory problems. The lead and zinc smelting plant, built in the 1960s, produced dangerous fumes containing lead, zinc, cadmium, and arsenic. Workers at the factory did not wear any protective clothing and did not even have glasses to shield them from the sparks and glare of the furnace. Conditions that would be immediately outlawed in any Western European country were a way of life for the factory's employees. Ironically, some of the lead produced was used to line the walls of Ceausescu's palace in Bucharest to protect a small elite in the event of a nuclear war or accident.

THE NEW ROMANIA

Romania is still coping with a new economic, social, and political way of life. In many ways the quality of life has improved dramatically. A new middle class has arisen that has the money to buy what was once affordable only by the rich—cars, mobile phones, imported goods. Where computers were previously hard to find, Internet use is on the rise. An estimated 18 percent of the population have access to the Internet. Even the Romanian government has gone electronic to develop closer links with the business world and its own people.

Still some old habits remain. Romanians still hoard what they can reuse—cardboard boxes, plastic bags, glass bottles. This is particularly true for many Romanians who have been left behind in the transition to a market economy, especially old-age pensioners as their pensions are low.

Parents of the bride at a ceremony held before the wedding that includes a forgiveness ritual in which the young couple formally ask their parents and relatives to forgive them for leaving behind their respective families.

WEDDINGS

Before 1989 many weddings were marked by an official ceremony at the local mayor's office followed by a simple church wedding. Since the revolution, however, there has been an increase in more elaborate traditional wedding ceremonies.

Couples tend to marry at a later age than in the past. Before 1989 a law ensured that college graduates had to work for three years outside the 12 largest cities in the country. This was mainly because the government wanted to control the location of the workforce and reduce the over-industrialization of large urban areas. Young graduates had little control over their immediate future, and college friends were frequently separated by being assigned to different parts of the country. This encouraged young people to marry quickly, to ensure they would be assigned together to a particular location.

In the countryside, weddings traditionally take place on a Sunday, and in some places the custom of announcing the marriage by a messenger on horseback is still observed. The bride is assisted by her maids of honor, while the best man helps the bridegroom prepare for the big event. On the day of the wedding, everyone has an appointed role: speakers at the ceremony; cooks; cup-bearers charged with maintaining a steady flow of drinks; musicians for pan pipes, dulcimers, and violins; and the best man, whose functions include carrying a colored pole decorated with handkerchiefs and bells during the wedding procession.

A wedding is an occasion for people to parade in traditional forms of dress, including the horseman with his handwoven saddle blankets. Women attend to most of the ceremonial details, including the headdresses. Married women cover their heads with a *naframa* (NE-frah-mah), a handkerchief of silk or cotton, while unmarried females will plait their hair and leave it uncovered. The bride's hair is braided, using techniques that have been passed down from mother to daughter, and is covered with a coronet decorated with flowers, semiprecious stones, and ribbons of various colors. The bridegroom wears a felt hat covered with feathers and flowers, and by tradition he is dressed in a white vest made from the skin of a young goat, decorated with strands of colored leather. He is clean-shaven, having had his beard cut by the best man as a mark of his passing bachelorhood.

Before the day of the wedding, a special large loaf of bread is baked for the marriage ceremony. The bride and groom take bites of this loaf between them, sharing the same spoon and plate, while they are showered with grains of corn and drops of water. The showering of the couple with the basics of life—corn and water—is a symbolic blessing and a wish for them to enjoy their future life together.

The modern wedding ceremony contains elements of traditional and religious rituals and Western-style weddings.

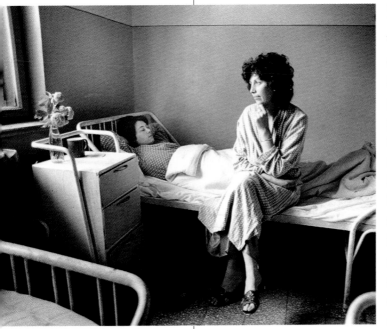

Above: **Two women share a hospital bed as one waits for and the other recovers from an abortion. Abortion is the most common method of birth control in Romania.**

Opposite: **Nurses preparing milk for AIDS-infected babies in the hospital. Although the United Nations and various humanitarian agencies have offered monetary and medical aid, the plight of these babies remains uncertain.**

THE ROLE OF WOMEN

Women especially suffered under the rule of Ceausescu because of the role they were forced to play in the government's population policy. The aim was to reach a population of 30 million by the year 2000, the belief being that a country's power rested on its industrial output, and hence its workforce. Every woman was required by law to have at least five children, and there were tax penalties for those with fewer than three children. Married women up to the age of 45 were subjected to compulsory monthly gynecological examinations to ensure that no illicit abortions had taken place. If they were pregnant, they were monitored to ensure they did not abort the baby.

Abortion and birth control for Romanian women under 45 years old were banned before 1989. After the bans were lifted in 1989, more than three abortions were recorded for each birth the next year. Recent statistics have shown that abortions are declining in number, but there are still more abortions than births in Romania today. Abortion still remains the main form of birth control because it is cheaper than buying contraceptives and is freely available.

In the workplace, women are paid less than men and are less likely to be in a managerial position. Research shows that women are the first to lose their jobs during an economic crisis. Budget cuts to social services and childcare have also hindered the progress of working women.

INNOCENT VICTIMS: THE CHILDREN OF ROMANIA

The government's drive to increase the country's population led to the birth of thousands of unwanted children. The human consequences of this, and the full horror of the government policy, only came to light after 1989 when the veil of secrecy was lifted. Romanian hospitals were full of both unwanted children and women still suffering the effects of illegal abortions. In 1989, after the fall of the Ceausescu regime, there were an estimated 130,000 children in Romania's orphanages. In the 1990s, the country was deluged with visits from European and North American adoption agencies, resulting in many Romanian infants and children leaving the country for a new home elsewhere.

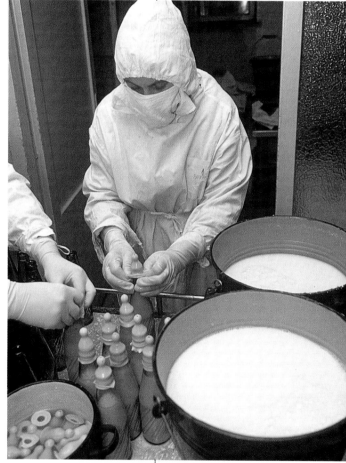

The general lack of food and welfare services meant that undernourished mothers gave birth to premature and underweight children. Many mothers were unable to feed their children with sufficient nutritious milk because the country could neither produce enough milk nor distribute it. As a result, hospitals had the task of intravenously feeding newborn infants with essential nutrients. In the past hospitals reused hypodermic needles to treat such children, thereby causing an AIDS epidemic among Romania's infants. In 1994 Romania had over 3,000 cases of children with AIDS, more than half of Europe's pediatric AIDS cases.

ROMANIA'S ORPHANS

Romania still has about 40,000 orphans today under the care of the government. Some of these orphans are a result of Ceasescu's population policy and food rationing and some are a result of Romania's current economic conditions. Since government subsidies for food have been withdrawn, poverty has become more widespread and thousands of families cannot afford to keep their new babies, abandoning them at orphanages around the country.

Adopting a Romanian child was popular among European and American childless families in the 1990s, especially after pictures of the miserable conditions orphans were kept in appeared in the West. Abuse of the adoption system soon became a major problem, and the adoption trade also became entangled with child prostitution and organ transplant rackets. Romanian children were also being sold on the Internet. In 2004 the Romanian government imposed a ban on all foreign adoptions except those by close relatives abroad. To some countries, such as the United States and Britain, the ban deprives Romanian orphans of a chance for a better life with a foreign family. The Romanian government, however, imposed the ban to align Romania with an existing European Union ban, which was introduced at the request of the EU in 2001 to protect Romania's orphans from child trafficking. The EU wants the ban to remain until Romania has tougher laws and better controls for the protection of its orphans.

SCHOOLED FOR EMPLOYMENT

Until the 1990s all schools were state schools run by the Communist government. Apart from private tutors, no form of private education was allowed by law. Education was compulsory for Romanian children between the ages of 7 and 14. Students could then choose to continue their education and would be urged to choose subjects considered suitable for them. Students who were more academically inclined were encouraged to follow subjects such as mathematics and physics, because these were subjects deemed to be of direct value to the state. Other students were trained in technical skills to prepare them to enter Romania's industrial and agricultural workforce. All aspects of the curriculum were rigidly controlled by the government, but subjects like history and literature were especially prone to ideological control. There was no room for views of history that conflicted with the political system in operation within the country.

Since 1989 private educational institutions have flourished alongside public schools. Schools are widely available in cities, but not in less accessible rural areas. The school attendance of children in rural areas is also much lower than in urban areas. Romania's education budget is low compared to the West, around 4 percent of the country's GDP. This has hindered the government's attempts at getting more children to attend school.

Romania has a high literacy rate of about 98 percent. School is free and compulsory for children from the ages of 7 to 14. The academic year is from October to June. Pre-education is available for children between 3 and 7 years of age.

Education is still compulsory for children up to Grade 9. Children in Grade 9 graduate with a *Certificat de Capacitate*, or certificate of capacity, when they pass their examinations. Their examination results will determine if they can enrol in one of these three branches of higher secondary education: theoretical, technological, or vocational. Vocational education includes vocational schools and apprentice schools. About 1.5 percent of secondary school students enter higher education each year.

Romania has 112 universities and institutions of higher learning. Fifty-four of these institutions are funded by the state. The most renowned universities are in Bucharest, Cluj, and Iasi. Medicine, law, and information technology are popular fields of study. Romania's oldest university is the University of Bucharest, founded in 1694.

Women washing clothes in the river. The more rural parts of Romania do not have running water.

LIFE IN THE COUNTRYSIDE

The Barbu family had farmed land near the city of Brasov in Transylvania for many generations. In 1948 a process of collectivization was begun by the government, and private ownership of land was abolished. Small farms were amalgamated to form large ones that were administered by the government. The Barbu land was farmed by workers who received a weekly wage, just like the Barbus' son, who chose to leave to work in a factory in a nearby city. In 1992 the 21 acres of land was returned to the son of the Barbu factory worker, who now owns 16 cows, 50 pigs, and over a hundred chickens. The new farmer supplements his income by growing grapes to make wine.

Such a story is typical of the dramatic changes taking place in the Romanian countryside, where nearly 47 percent of the country's population

PEASANT HOMES

The typical rural farmhouse is small and varies in color according to the geographical location. In Moldavia and Walachia they are usually white, while in Transylvania a mixture of colors is more common. Whatever the color, the roof is usually covered with red tiles, corrugated metal, or small, flat pieces of rectangular wood known as shingles. The staircase connecting the upper floor with the ground floor is often built on the outside of the house. Adjacent to the domestic building are various sheds for storing animal feed and winter fuel such as wood.

Farming families in Romania are far more self-sufficient than their counterparts in Western Europe, and they grow a variety of vegetables and food for their own consumption. Often they also supply food to family members in urban areas, which are faced with inflationary prices.

Many peasant homes have a front porch, in the manner of the North American frontier homestead. Furniture inside the home is likely to be made of beautifully crafted wood. Colorful rugs, tablecloths, and mats embroidered by women in the household are proudly displayed. Cooking and heating are usually provided by means of a wood or gas stove. Electricity is available for lighting, but a refrigerator is not as common as it is in North American homes.

lives and works. The political revolution of 1989 took place in the towns and cities, but in the countryside a radical social revolution has seen more than 85 percent of arable land returned to its former owners.

The rules governing the privatization of land allow individuals to reclaim land that was owned and farmed by their ancestors up to four generations back. What this means is that a young woman who is living and working in Bucharest today may, if it can be established that her great-grandfather once had a farm of 25 acres (10 hectares) or less, claim ownership of the family land. She can either farm it or put it up for sale. In practice, the whole process of verifying claims and settling conflicting claims is a complex business. There are over 13,000 villages in the country, and most of them are undergoing a change of identity as they once again become the focus of life for local and privately-owned farms.

Romania's countryside is sparsely populated, 124 people per square mile (48 people per square km) as compared to 1,244 per square mile (480 people per square km) in urban areas.

RELIGION

IN THE 1992 CENSUS, 99.8 percent of the population officially declared a religion, with the vast majority of Romanians (nearly 87 percent) belonging to the Romanian Orthodox Church. Protestants are the next largest denomination at 6.8 percent with Catholics making up 5.6 percent of the population. A small number of Muslims also live in Romania.

The Romanian Orthodox Church is one branch of the Eastern Orthodox Church, which is a group of self-governing churches that recognizes the honorary primacy of the Patriarch of Constantinople. The role of religion in Romania has changed dramatically since the 1989 revolution.

Left: **The Orthodox Cathedral at Sighisoara by the Tirnava Mare river.**

Opposite: **The Orthodox Cathedral in Alba Iulia, built in 1921–22 for the coronation of King Ferdinand I and Quen Marie.**

The lighting of candles during prayer is an essential part of the liturgy of the Eastern Orthodox Church.

EASTERN ORTHODOXY

Eastern Orthodoxy is the body of Christianity that follow the faith and practices defined by the universal church. The term universal applies to the whole church before the split between the Western and Eastern churches in 1054. When the Eastern and Western churches broke off contact, the Eastern churches kept the term orthodox as a sign of faithfulness.

The reasons for the split of the universal church are numerous and complicated. They are related to the division of the Roman Empire into an eastern and western half, centered in the cities of Constantinople (present-day Istanbul) and Rome respectively.

Originally the entire Christian church worked together to establish a consensus on matters of doctrine. However, the two branches of Christianity evolved in different directions because of the culture and philosophy of the lands in which they developed. The Western church, which developed in Rome and parts of Western Europe, leaned toward a more legalistic approach, while Eastern Christianity, which developed in Greece, the Middle East, Eastern Europe, Russia, and northern Africa, espoused a more mystical theology. During the ninth century, conflict involving differences of opinion over doctrinal matters widened, leading to the Great Schism of 1045. This is considered to be the start of the division between the two churches. By the 1450s, when Constantinople fell to the Muslim Turks, the split was permanent.

ORTHODOX BELIEFS

The Eastern Orthodox Church (also referred to as the Byzantine Church), like Protestantism, rejects the belief that the Pope is infallible. Roman Catholics adhere to the notion that when it comes to theological matters, the Pope cannot make a mistake. Unlike Protestantism, however, the Eastern Orthodox church believes in transubstantiation. That is, it believes that in the celebration of the Eucharist, or Holy Communion, ordinary bread and wine are transformed into the body and blood of Christ. Thus, the Holy Communion is the high point of the liturgy of the Eastern Orthodox Church.

The Romanian Orthodox Church, in common with all Eastern Orthodox churches, gives a central place to icons, or holy images. A believer in a church goes up to the iconostasis—the wall of paintings that separates the sanctuary from the nave—and kisses the icons. On the feast day of a particular saint, the icon of that saint is displayed on the lectern where the faithful pay their respects by a kiss and a bow, and then make the sign of the cross before rejoining the congregation.

At home, a Romanian Orthodox family usually has an icon hanging in the eastern corner of the living room and another in the bedroom. Traditionally, a guest on entering a room first greets the icon by making the sign of the cross and bowing to it.

On Sunday mornings and at the grand Easter services, which are more important than Christmas festivals, Orthodox churches are filled with the smoke of incense and hundreds of burning candles. It creates a mystical atmosphere, especially when accompanied by the sonorous music of singing choirs invisible to the congregation.

Icons adorn the walls separating the sanctuary from the congregation.

MYSTICISM

One way of appreciating the difference between the Orthodox religious experience and that of Western Christianity is by understanding the importance of mysticism in the Eastern Orthodox Church. By comparison, it has been observed, Western Christianity is legalistic in some of its concepts and beliefs, due perhaps to the influence of ancient Roman society's emphasis on law. The Eastern Orthodox Church, by contrast, is more open to the influence of mystical strands of thought in Middle Eastern religious philosophy.

For example, the act of penance—by which the sinner regains spiritual purity through obligatory prayer—is seen in the Orthodox Church as a road to sanctity; in the Roman Catholic Church, penance is often seen and experienced as an act of compensation. In the Orthodox Church, the doctrine of purgatory—which allows a sinner to be saved even after death by undergoing a temporary state somewhere between heaven and hell—was never incorporated into mainstream beliefs.

In the Roman Catholic Church, salvation through purgatory has a judicial component: the sinner could be redeemed by acts of prayer and intervention by the Church. This idea had little in common with the major themes of Orthodox belief: sanctification, rebirth, recreation, and resurrection. Also in the Orthodox Church, God's love is stressed more than God's justice and this is apparent in the way Judgment Day is perceived. There is little emphasis on the individual's right to salvation, nor is there any question of a person's achievements being able to influence the act of admittance into heaven. Instead, there is an extraordinary confidence in the notion of grace, the idea that love is the only necessary passport to eternal life with God.

ICONS

The golden background of an icon represents the heavenly aura that surrounds the holy figure.

In the Orthodox Church, an icon is traditionally regarded as a kind of window between the earthly and the celestial worlds; a window through which an inhabitant of the celestial world—a saint, or Christ himself—looks down into our earthly one. The image recorded in the icon is a sacred one because of the belief that the true features of the heavenly spirit have somehow been imprinted in a two-dimensional way on the icon. This belief in the sacred nature of an icon was developed by early religious scholars in the eighth and ninth centuries into the concept of incarnation, meaning that God appears in human form. The idea was that Christ becomes incarnate in the very materials of the icon—the wood, plaster, egg white, and oils. This belief never became orthodox dogma, but it helps explain the extraordinary reverence accorded to icons in the religion.

Icons have a curious archaic strangeness that often makes them appear mysterious even to the nonbeliever. As a form of art, icons have no concept of authorship. This is one of the radical differences between the art of the icon and the art of Western Christianity. For centuries, the Eastern Orthodox Church has been content to repeat certain types of sacred images so that only a specialist could assign an icon to a specific century.

The craft of producing icons was done in monasteries, with a group of monks working together on one icon. One monk might work on the eyes or hair, while another would devote himself to painting the robes of the figure being represented. Icon painters (iconographers) prepared themselves for painting through fasting, prayer, and Holy Communion, because it was believed that to paint Christ better, one must have a close relationship with God. Today, some iconographers are specially trained laypeople.

During the eighth and ninth centuries, partly through the influence of Islam, an opposition to images in worship began to pervade the Eastern Orthodox Church. During the annual Feast of Orthodoxy, instituted in A.D. 842, the entire Orthodox Church celebrates and honors the victory of those who supported the use of icons during worship over the iconoclasts—those who opposed the use of icons.

Images of saints on the walls and ceiling of a Romanian church.

An offering of food and prayers for those who died or suffered in the 1989 revolution.

CHURCH BUILDINGS

Some of Romania's older churches are famous for their exterior frescos and are themselves recognized as works of art. The images that adorn the interior of an Eastern Orthodox church have fixed places. They appear in the sanctuary, the iconostasis, and the dome.

Even within one of these places, the order of the images follows a traditional pattern that has been observed for centuries. The pattern of icons on the iconostasis is an example: the annunciation of the Virgin Mary is depicted on the Royal or Holy gates; the icon of Christ is always to the right of the Royal doors; and Mary, with the infant Jesus in her arms, is to the left; John the Baptist would be to the right of Christ; and to the left of Mary appears the icon of the saint to whom the church is dedicated.

The Archangels Gabriel and Michael are pictured on the deacon doors, which are to the right and left of the Royal gates. Occasionally the four evangelists are also shown on the Royal gates. The Last Supper may also be depicted above the gates. If the church is large enough, icons of the apostles and prophets will be displayed. Again there is a hierarchy that dictates the order in which figures appear. The first row contains apostles, followed by a row of saints and martyrs, then prophets, and finally the patriarchs of the Old Testament are found along the fourth row. Above the central door of the iconostasis, there is usually a representation of Christ on the throne, with Mary and John the Baptist to the right and left respectively. Apart from churches, there are innumerable Orthodox monasteries, many of which are regarded as works of major artistic and architectural interest.

RELIGION BEFORE 1989

Romania was officially an atheist country under Communist rule, although some churches were allowed to function and it was not against the law to practice certain religions. For instance, the Orthodox Church of Romania was allowed to function as long as it cooperated with the Communist government. Still, its activities were strictly supervised by the government, and active churchgoing was discouraged. However, many churches, such as those belonging to ethnic minorities, were disbanded for refusing to cooperate with government policies. Some religious leaders were also arrested and jailed for refusing to obey the government's requirements.

An issue that upset many people was the Communist dictate that Christmas Day was no longer a holiday, but a regular working day. Some protests were organized over the years but the authorities were always quick to put them down.

RELIGION AFTER 1989

The revolution occurred during the month of December and the Ceausescus were executed on December 25. To many people outside Eastern Europe, the idea of executing someone on Christmas Day seemed bizarre, but to many Romanians the execution and the date of the event were appropriate.

Christmas Day in 1989 was a surprisingly fine day, with a winter sun bringing a little warmth to an otherwise harsh winter. Many Romanians remember the day of the execution and the weather as having a mystical significance: the Ceausescu regime was over, and a new beginning beckoned. After the execution, the death penalty was abolished and churches were filled with worshipers, most of whom had not attended a church service for many years.

The Romanian Constitution guarantees religious freedom, and the Romanian government generally respects the people's rights to practice any religion they choose. But the country's laws give the government a strong say over religious life. For instance the government can prohibit certain religious organizations from operating within Romania.

A Moldavian stone church with a wooden steeple in the Bistrita valley. The architecture probably reflects the influence of the Turks in the 14th and 15th centuries.

POLITICAL PRIESTS

Before 1989, churches were not outlawed, but they were carefully monitored by the state to ensure that they did not upset the status quo. Unlike other Communist countries, the Ceausescu regime paid special attention to its relations with the Orthodox Church because the religion was a dominant part of many people's lives, especially in the villages. It

A RELIGIOUS RESISTANCE

The Hungarian Reformed Church of Timisoara was initially composed mainly of elderly women. When Laszlo Tokes became its pastor, he increased and broadened the church membership, and invigorated its appeal by speaking out against the government. One Sunday in September 1989, uniformed police formed a human barrier to the members of the congregation in front of the church. A court order for Tokes' eviction from the church was signed by the local authorities and was due to take place on December 15, 1989. But a few days before this Tokes had told his congregation: "If anyone would like to see an illegal conviction, I invite him to come and watch."

On the night of December 15, members of the Hungarian Reformed Church maintained a vigil outside Tokes' house to prevent him from being arrested. The next day the vigil turned into a major demonstration, and the ensuing clash between citizens and the police precipitated protests in other parts of Romania. Within days the whole country was in turmoil and unrest, and nothing was ever the same again.

was made clear to priests and religious authorities that they were under observation and had to accept the government's authority if they wanted to retain their positions. This situation introduced politics into religion, and priests were forced into a political role.

A number of priests—the majority, according to many Romanians—accepted the government's authority. Stories of priests colluding with the internal security police were common, and it was frequently observed that a priest could not be relied upon to keep any matter a secret from the government. In effect, some priests were accused of being spies, and since 1989 they have had the task of regaining the respect of the people.

Other priests, however, saw their role under Ceausescu quite differently. For them, their duty lay in challenging the government. The priests or religious authorities who were brave enough to challenge the government were harassed or murdered by the Securitate. The spark that ignited the revolution concerned a Romanian church leader in the Transylvanian town of Timisoara. The leader, pastor Laszlo Tokes, was being harassed by the security police, and his congregation's determination to resist his arrest by the police led to an outbreak of local resistance in Timisoara and other parts of Romania. This resistance eventually culminated in the overthrow of the government in December 1989.

VAMPIRES AND WEREWOLVES

A belief in vampires existed in Romania and neighboring parts of southeastern Europe long before the Dracula story appeared at the end of the 19th century. Vampirism is related to the notion that the soul may not always leave a person's body after death. A vampire is a corpse that remains undead because its spirit still resides in the body, which does not decompose, no matter how long it has been buried in the ground.

One reason for believing such an occurrence is that when a person died in what might be believed to be an obvious state of sin—suicide, for example—the soul is supposedly unable to leave the body in the normal way. Romanians used to particularly fear death through hanging because of the notion that constriction of the neck forced the soul downward and hence prevented its escape from the body. It is a custom to cover mirrors in the home of the recently deceased, in case the departing spirit becomes trapped upon seeing its reflection.

Vampires are feared because they are thought to return at night to the village and the homes where they once lived. Unchristened babies are thought to be vulnerable because they could be made into vampires. Two nights of the year are especially prone to vampire visitations: St. George's Day (April 23) and the night before St. Andrew's Day (November 29). There is a belief that offerings of food and drink must be made available on those days, and that garlic helps to repel vampires. The idea of the vampire biting the neck of its victim and sucking blood is partly a literary invention; in Romanian folklore, a touch, or even a glance, from a vampire is enough to bring about death.

Various stories have tried to explain the belief in vampires. For example, in the past, cases of premature burials were common because there was no sure way of determining death, hence the existence of the living "dead." What is evident is that the belief in vampirism has been a part of Romanian folklore for many centuries, and a willingness to accept the idea can still be found among the more superstitious people in the countryside.

In Romanian Roma folklore, it is believed that vampires can also function during part of the day, exactly at midday when there is no shadow cast by the sun. For that short duration, Roma consider it unsafe to travel out in the open because the vampire influence is potently present and poses a threat to ordinary mortals. Roma also believe that only a vampire corpse of their own undead can threaten them; the vampires of non-Roma ignore them and can in turn be ignored.

Like the vampire phenomenon, a belief in werewolves has long been part of traditional Romanian folklore. It was once a common tradition throughout Europe, but has largely died out and, unlike vampirism, has virtually no hold upon the imagination of even superstitious Romanians. Rational explanations for were-wolves include the medical condition of lycanthropy (an unreasonable and obsessive belief that one is a wolf); the infrequent disease of erythropoietic porphyria, which results in inflamed and itchy skin after short exposures to sunlight; and hirsutism, which causes the sufferer to develop excessive growth of body and facial hair.

An actor dresses up for the role of Dracula.

LANGUAGE

A STORY TOLD FOR AMUSEMENT in Romania recounts how a young farmer from Walachia visited Italy and returned home to tell how the Italians spoke his own tongue, "but badly!" Apart from expressing the pride that Romanians have in their own culture, the story also reveals the fact that Romanian is a Romance language with very close links to Latin.

People who are fluent in Italian and French are able to understand many words and phrases in Romanian, even though the language has also been influenced by non-Romance tongues such as Greek, Turkish, Hungarian, and Slavonic. Educated Romanians speak English, French, and German as well as Romanian. The chief minority language is Magyar, the language of ethnic Hungarians. Other languages spoken include German, Romany, Serbian, Ukrainian, Slovak, Czech, Bulgarian, and Turkish. National television and radio broadcasts are made in Hungarian and German during set periods of each day.

Left: **A man adjusts the lead type on a printing press.**

Opposite: **A newspaper stand in Bucharest.**

ROMANIAN WORDS & PHRASES

Hello	*buna ziua*	(BOON-a ZYOO-ah)
How are you?	*ce mai faci*	(chay my FAHtch)
My name is …	*ma numesc …*	(mah noo-MEHSK)
What is your name?	*cum te cheama*	(kum teh KIA-mah)
Yes	*da*	(DA)
No	*nu*	(NOOH)
Please	*poftiti*	(POF-teets)
Good morning	*buna dimineata*	(BOON-a di-mi-nee-AT-sa)
Goodnight	*noapte buna*	(nop-tay BOON-a)
Goodbye	*la revedere*	(la reve-DE-re)
God be with you	*domnul sa te aiba in paza*	(DOM-nul suh tay AY-ba in PAH-zuh)

ROMANIAN LANGUAGE

There is some disagreement among linguists over the origin and composition of the Romanian language. While the structure of the language is clearly Latinate, some words have Slavic, Turkish, and Hungarian origins. These influences reflect the political history of Romania.

Romanian nouns have three genders: masculine, feminine, and neuter. The plural of nouns usually ends in "—i," "—uri," or "—e," as in *case* (CAH-se; houses), and *copaci* (CO-PAH-CHI; trees). Adjectives are usually placed after the word they describe, and pronouns change their form slightly to agree with the gender of the noun.

The usual rule for pronunciation is that words are stressed on the syllable next to the last. For example, the word for money is *ban* and it is pronounced BAHN. Another important pronunciation rule is that all letters are pronounced. The word for food is *mincare* and it is pronounced mahn-KHAR-ay.

When words end in consonants, the stress falls mostly on the last syllable. Unlike the English language, two vowels coming together are pronounced separately and do not combine to form new sounds.

LANGUAGE ISSUES

Language is viewed by some people in Romania as a political issue. Before 1989, the Communist Party was committed to a policy of Romanization. Bilingual inscriptions on public buildings were replaced with Romanian texts, and in one Transylvanian town, Cluj-Napoca, the Latin inscription on a monument to the Hungarian King Matyas was replaced with a Romanian one. Some Hungarian young people demonstrated, and the police were called in.

In the Ceausescu era, minority-language edu-

Many Romanians can converse in a variety of languages, including German, English, and French, in addition to the Romanian language.

cation and literature were severely restricted. For instance, the Hungarian-language university set up in Transylvania to provide higher education for ethnic Hungarians in Romania was closed down in 1959 during the communist regime.

German, which is spoken in parts of western Romania, and the language of the Roma, Romany, were also discriminated against. Today, more Romanians, and not just those of German descent, are learning German so that they can do business with people in other parts of Europe.

THE MINORITIES SPEAK UP

Romania's constitution expressly outlaws any kind of discrimination against minority languages, and Article 32 affirms the right of minorities to learn their mother tongue and to be educated in that language. In Transylvania, road signs now have to appear in both Romanian and Hungarian, but this law is not often enforced. While the government has made some effort to encourage the use and growth of minority languages, cost is one of the reasons why it is unable to contribute more. Thus minority activist groups belonging to the Roma and ethnic Hungarians, for instance, have teamed up with non-governmental organizations to promote the use and learning of their respective languages. Examples of such cooperation is the monetary support given to ethnic Hungarian parents who send their children to Hungarian language schools and an increase in the wages of university and college lecturers who teach in Hungarian.

But a new law currently under consideration may curtail such activities. It proposes a quota system in which schools with fewer than 200 students will be closed. Ethnic Hungarians intend to overcome this obstacle by gathering their students and providing transport to send them to Hungarian language schools that remain open.

A MIXTURE OF LANGUAGES

In the capital of Bucharest and in some other towns, it is common to hear German, Bulgarian, Turkish, or Serbian being spoken. Over the centuries, a number of words have entered the Romanian language from other cultures. The word *bai* (baa-I), for example, is a Hungarian word meaning trouble, as is the word *hotar* (ho-TAR), which means border.

Hungarian is a unique language, classified as a member of the Finno-Ugric family of languages, bearing little in common with any other

language. Its nearest linguistic relative is Finnish, but for all practical purposes the two languages are quite distinct. Hungarian is regarded as a difficult language to learn. It is an agglutinating language, which means its vocabulary arises from a number of root-words that are modified and altered to express different ideas and shades of meaning.

Slavic words make up between 5 percent and 10 percent of Romanian vocabulary. There are also Albanian and Greek influences. The centuries during which Romania came under the influence of the Turkish empire has also left its mark on the Romanian language. Examples of Turkish words are *bacsis* (baak-SHISH) meaning tip, as in tipping a waiter.

The Roma of Romania also have their own language, Romany, which until recently had no tradition of writing. The first Romanian-Romany dictionary appeared after 1989.

ARTS

ROMANIA HAS A RICH CULTURE. The performance arts of theater, dance, music, and film have contributed their share of great artists. The impressive visual arts range from frescos in centuries-old buildings, paintings, and sculpture, to traditional works such as carvings, crafts, elaborately embroidered costumes, and skillfully-woven carpets.

CLASSICAL MUSIC

Classical music in Romania does not have the elitist associations found elsewhere. It was readily available to everyone, since Western music was frowned on during the years of Communist rule. Generous state sponsorship meant the development of at least one philharmonic orchestra or opera house in each major town, and it ensured that ticket prices were affordable for ordinary people. After 1989 subsidies were withdrawn, making it difficult for many companies to survive, as the cost of running an orchestra is quite high.

Romantic composer George (JOR-je) Enescu (1881–1955) is one of Romania's greatest musicians and his influence is still felt in Romania. Enescu was a composer, violinist, pianist, and conductor of world fame. He is well known for integrating themes of peasant folk music into his own classical compositions, and his *Romanian Rhapsodies* is noted for its haunting traditional melodies of rural Romanian music. Enescu was a highly respected violin teacher. The American violinist Yehudi Menuhin was one of his outstanding pupils. Another world-renowned Romanian musician is the late Munich Philharmonic conductor, Sergiu Celibidache.

Above: **The Symphonic Orchestra of the George Enescu Philharmony.**

Opposite: **The Music Museum located in Bucharest was formerly the house of musician George Enescu.**

The sound produced by the *bacium* is similar to that of the horn.

FOLK MUSIC

Folk music is the strongest and richest form of music in the country and is among the most enduring and fruitful tradition of folk music in Europe. A diversity of styles that stretch back centuries have been passed down and improvised from one generation to the next. Only in the last 30 years or so has a sustained effort been made to record this rich heritage.

Folk music is still part of the living culture of the people and is enjoyed at weddings, funerals, and various festivities where dance and music are customary. Different regions of the country evolved their own special forms, for example, *doina* (doi-NAH) music is associated with Maramures in the northwest of the country. *Doina* music has been compared with American blues because of its soulful and melancholy rhythms. In the more mountainous parts of the country, the music tends to relate to the working lives of the shepherds, and folk instruments such as panpipes and the *buchium* (BOO-chium), a long wooden wind instrument rather like an alpenhorn, are used.

TRANSYLVANIAN MUSIC

The racial mix of ethnic Romanians and Hungarians in Transylvania has made the region particularly rich in folk music. When Hungary was occupied by the Ottoman Turks for 150 years, Transylvania remained an independent principality with its cultural identity intact. Hence, in the early 20th century, the famous Hungarian composer Béla Bartok (1881–1945) went there in search of the Asiatic roots of his country's music, which had been lost in Hungary itself. The old village settlement patterns survived, and the lack of contact with the outside world during the Ceausescu period helped to preserve the region's unique musical heritage and traditions.

The Bucharest-Moldavian quartet performs.

Transylvania, however, is not a mere enclave for Hungarian music. It is a unique blend of different traditions. It is not the same as Hungarian music in Hungary or Romanian music in the rest of Romania, but only a trained ear can differentiate the melodies and rhythms of the two cultures. The typical Transylvanian ensemble is a string trio: a viola, a double bass, and a violin that is modified to amplify the sound of the ordinary instrument. Such bands frequently play at weddings and they need to be heard above the loud noise of the festivities. Sometimes another violist joins the band to add volume and contribute to a fuller sound. The *kontra-violin*, an instrument similar to the viola but with only three strings and a flat bridge that enables chords to be played, is often used in the ensemble, and it gives Transylvanian music its distinctive sound.

Most of the folk musicians are Roma, who have a rich music tradition. In Transylvania, the Roma have created a distinct musical form combining Hungarian, Romanian, and Roma melodies.

MUSIC ON THE FRINGE

Such is the richness of Romanian folk music that there are small pockets of the country that preserve their own unique musical heritage. A remarkable example of this is the area known as Gyimes, a mountainous pastoral area between Moldavia and Transylvania. Ethnic Hungarians live here, having migrated across the mountains many centuries ago, and their music is heard nowhere else in the country. It has a wild and reckless sound that outsiders associate with gypsies and is played on just two instruments: a violin and a *gardon* (gar-DON), the latter being shaped like a cello, but played in the manner of a percussion instrument, with the strings being hit by a small stick.

LITERATURE

As far back as the 14th century in Romania monks would copy religious manuscripts, usually in Slavonic. The Romanian language only came into use in the mid-16th century. But it was only in 1860, when Romania officially switched to the Latin alphabet from the Cyrillic version, that modern Romanian literature was born.

Some of Romania's most famous 19th century writers and poets include Vasile Alecsandri, Ion Creanga, Mihai Eminescu, and I.L. Caragiale. Creanga is known for his humorous stories. His most important work is *Amintiri din Copilarie (Childhood Memories)*. Probably the best-known Romanian poet is Eminescu, who died tragically at age 39 from ill health. Some of his more famous poems include *Luceafarul* (translated as *Evening Star*, *Lucifer*, or *Hyperion*) and *Scrisorile* (*Epistles*). Marin Preda is one of the more well-known post-World War II writers. He is known for his award-winning *The Great Lonely One* (1972). Marin Sorescu is also a famous poet and dramatist.

A trend that emerged after 1989 is that of the documentary literature, which detail events over a period of time. One of the most famous in this genre is *The Silent Escape: Three Thousand Days in Romanian Prisons* by Lena Constante. It is a first-person account of the author's 12 years of solitary confinement in a Romanian prison—the longest by any woman in Romania—after she was charged falsely with espionage.

PAINTED MONASTERIES

The region of northern Moldavia has a number of medieval monasteries with painted exterior walls. The wall paintings, like the monasteries, date from the 15th and 16th centuries, and were a form of church propaganda designed for the illiterate peasants. The paintings vividly illustrate both the punishments for sinners and the rewards due to the faithful in the next world; as such, they taught the peasants to obey and fear their spiritual and political masters. But the quality of the artwork goes beyond crude propaganda, and the range of the images is both startling and sophisticated. Today they are regarded as major artistic achievements.

The spiritual architect of the painted monasteries was voivode Stephen the Great, a celebrated military commander under whose rule, from 1457 to 1504, a number of monasteries and churches were built. The exterior frescos represent one of the most precious examples of medieval art: biblical tableaux recording the fears and aspirations of society in the Middle Ages.

The Moldovita Monastery was built in 1532 and painted in 1537. It was founded by Petru Rares, the ruler of Moldavia at that time. His throne, which is considered to be a piece of classic 16th century Moldavian ornamental art, can be found in this monastery.

SUCEVITA MONASTERY

One of the most artistically adorned monasteries is Sucevita (Su-che-VEE-tza), one of the five churches built in Suceava County in the 15th century. On the exterior of the north wall is a fresco entitled *The Ladder of St. John from Sinai*, which shows angels helping people climb the ladder to paradise, while sinners fall through the rungs into the arms of demons. On the southern wall, the Virgin Mary is painted beneath a shining red veil, next to a frieze of scholars. One of the scholars is the ancient Greek philosopher Plato who carries a small coffin with bones on his head. This may have been interpreted as a way of thinking about the inevitability of death. Inside the monastery the Last Judgment is illustrated, and there is a series of grisly reminders of how various saints and martyrs were tortured and persecuted for their faith.

VORONET MONASTERY

This monastery, built in 1488 by Stephen the Great, is most famous for a wide expanse of paintings covering the entire west wall. Particularly, *The Last Judgment* is generally considered the finest example of Romanian church art. The central figure of Christ sits above a chair that has the Latin inscription meaning Toll Gates of the Air, where the recently deceased are judged and sent to their final destinations. By the side of Christ are painted a whole host of figures: Adam and Eve, Moses, martyrs, and the prophets. On each side of the deceased are those in limbo, recognizable by their turbans and tall hats. They were depicted as the Turks and Tatars, who were the very real enemies of Moldavia in the 15th century. Farther down, two angels are seen blowing on the *buchium*, a long wind instrument, which is a signal for graves to open and wild animals to appear bearing the remains of the bodies they have devoured.

The various symbolic images would have resonated with meaning for a 15th century audience; for example, only the deer does not carry human limbs, for in Romanian folklore this animal stands for innocence. Many of the frescos are painted blue, and one of the shades of blue used extensively has been given a distinct name—Voronet blue.

ROMANIAN ARTISTS

The likenesses of the sculptor Brancusi and the poet Eminescu adorn Romania's banknotes. In this way, the country honors its artists.

Eugène Ionesco, born in Romania in 1912, was educated in Bucharest and Paris, where he settled prior to World War II. He is most famous for his one-act plays that are characteristic examples of surrealist theater. Having spent so much of his life in Paris, he is often regarded more as a French artist than a Romanian one. Similarly, the poet Tristan Tzara (1896–1963) was born in Romania but spent most of his life outside the country. Despite this, both these surrealist artists show, in their rejection of realism and logic, an affinity with the unreal and mysterious world of the traditional Romanian folktale.

The work of the poet Mihai Eminescu (1850–89), on the other hand, is regarded as the epitome of the Romanian soul in its more idealistic mood. Influenced by the European Romantics, his poetry extols the virtue of solitary reflection and stoicism by an individual when faced with disappointment and failure in personal, and especially romantic, life. Even though 1989 was the centenary of his death, the event was passed over with little notice—typical of the way in which the Communist regime prevented any individual, apart from Ceausescu himself, from enjoying too much fame. In 1990, a year after the revolution, far more effort went into recognizing the country's most respected poet.

In the field of sculpture, the Romanian Constantin Brancusi (1876–1957) is world famous. He was a carpenter's apprentice before leaving to study at the Bucharest Academy. In 1904, he left for Paris on foot, having insufficient money to travel, and he lived in the French capital for the rest of his life. He turned down an invitation to join Auguste Rodin's studio, although the influence of Rodin is apparent in his *Sleeping Muse* of 1910, the first of many characteristic, highly-polished, egg-shaped sculptures. He worked with stone, marble, steel, and wood, and many of his highly-regarded works are on display in museums in the United States and France. Brancusi was born in the countryside and spent part of his young life as a shepherd. His love for nature is clear in his art, in which he fuses natural forms with the themes of modern art.

FOLK ART

Present-day Romanian folk art is mainly confined to the northwest region of Maramures. In fairly remote villages, the residents have retained features of their culture and lifestyle that have not changed for centuries. It is one of the few parts of Europe where people still wear folk costumes daily and where

Woodcarver's house with a traditional gateway.

their adherence to the Eastern Orthodox Church is mingled with a far older paganism that is expressed in a belief in spiritualism.

The most artistic form of folk art is the woodcraft adorning village buildings. Doorways and windows of homes are carefully carved with decorative motifs, and the entry to a farmhouse is also marked by an elaborately carved wooden gateway. Beautiful and intricate carvings are also found in the woodcraft of the 18th-century wooden churches scattered across rural Romania. Hungarians and Germans living in Romania also have their own folk art traditions and costumes.

MIORITA

The folk ballad *Miorita* (mee-O-REE-tza), or *Little Ewe Lamb*, speaks symbolically of the Romanian character and the belief that death is not the end but the start of a beautiful journey. It tells the story of three shepherds, one of whom discovers a plot by the others to kill him, but instead of resisting, he accepts his death as an act of fate and mortality as a fact of life. While awaiting his fate, he asks his favorite sheep, Miorita, to tell his mother that he has married a beautiful princess (Death):

I have gone to marry
A princess—my bride.
Firs and maple trees
Were my guests; my priests
Were the mountains high,
Fiddlers, birds that fly.
Torchlight, stars on high.

FOLK BALLADS

The writer Ion Creanga (1837–89) is little known outside of Romania, where he is renowned as a storyteller and writer. *Childhood Memories* is his most famous work and in it he recalls his own childhood when folk ballads were an important influence. Creanga himself employs the language and imagery of traditional folktales in his fiction, and his work evokes the peculiar nature of a folk art that has now virtually disappeared from Europe.

Popular ballads flourished in Romania between the 16th and 19th centuries and were told to the accompaniment of music on a lute, a zither, or a cimpoi (CHIM-poy), an instrument resembling a bagpipe. Although the vocabulary is quite simple, the ballads are full of verbal rhymes, metaphors, and the personification of natural forms, such as an oak tree or a bird. Such ballads evoke a world where the bond between people and nature was far closer than it is today.

THE CINEMA

The potential of cinema as an art form was quickly recognized in Romania. In the early decades of the last century, Bucharest was one of the film centers of Eastern Europe, and many artists turned to the cinema as their preferred art form.

The Romanian animator Ion Popescu-Gopo won a major award at the 1957 Cannes Film Festival for a short animated film called *Brief History*. The story linked the traditional folktales of Romania with the new form of the cinema.

The allegorical approach was developed in a different direction in the late 1970s due to the repressive censorship system in the country. Film directors were forced to conceal their dissident mood under the guise of film parables. These could be decoded by an audience who understood the social and political meaning behind various innocent-looking images. Such films became known as iceberg movies because their true meaning lay hidden and what was seen was only a small part of the message.

A scene from a film directed by Romanian Catalina Buzoianu, and starring Valeria Seciu and Stefan Iordache.

The fall of Communism and the transition period has provided Romanian moviemakers with much material. Lucian Pintilie is a renowned Romanian director whose works have been shown at the prestigious Cannes Festival in France. His 1992 film *The Oak* dealt with life under Ceausescu, while his most recent film *Niki et Flo* dramatizes the attitudes of post-1989 Romanians toward their country, emigration to the United States, family, and aging. Another award-winning film is *Occident* by Christian Muhgiu that also discusses life after 1989 and Romanians' desire to seek a better life in the West. Maia Morgenstern, who acted the part of Mary the mother of Jesus in the 2004 movie *The Passion of the Christ*, is one of Romania's best-known actresses.

107

LEISURE

WHAT IS BROADLY DESCRIBED as folk culture is an intrinsic part of Romanian life. This is so despite a process of intense industrialization that has lasted for many decades and has endangered the country's root identity. One way of appreciating the effects of this process is by looking at the way leisure time is employed among different sections of Romanian society. The leisure activities of a traditional rural community that is reasonably self-sufficient are vastly different from those of an urban community in a modern industrial city.

Opposite: **Poiana Brasov is a premier ski resort in Romania.**

Below: **Mamaia, the Black Sea beach resort just north of the city of Constanta, is popular with Romanians and tourists.**

Young members of the Patriotic Guards in one of the numerous parades staged during Ceausescu's regime. It was said that when he visited China in 1971, he was so impressed with Chinese mass displays of patriotism that when he instituted "mass culture" programs in 1975, they were modelled on the Chinese propaganda techniques.

COMPULSORY LEISURE

Under Ceausescu it was official policy to create the New Man—a model citizen emerging from a forced mixing of workers from agricultural and proletarian backgrounds. This new hybrid citizen was to be the building block for Romania's bright new future in the 21st century. To create this New Man, Ceausescu used a systematization policy in which whole villages were razed to the ground, and the residents resettled in concrete agroindustrial complexes. Traditional patterns of work and leisure were destroyed and replaced by an imposed regimentation that bore little resemblance to the indigenous culture of the people.

An example of enforced leisure was the *Cintarea Romaniei* (can-TAH-rah RO-ma-NIEA) (*Singing Romania*) displays that took place in huge stadiums or on open hillsides to which hundreds of peasants had been transported. This effort was to make the event appear natural and authentic. The people were dressed in folk costumes and performed song and dance routines that were supposed to represent people relaxing and enjoying themselves. Such shows were recorded and televised across the country on weekends. Therefore Romanians relaxing at home and watching television had little choice but to watch such an unedifying diet of entertainment.

LEISURE TIME IN VILLAGES

In the more remote parts of Romania, which managed to escape the systematization policy of the previous Communist government, small pockets of communities survive that seem to have more in common with the Middles Ages than with the 20th century. There, the traditional way of work and leisure has continued fairly unchanged. For instance, many people still wear traditional costumes as everyday dress and not just for festive occasions. Even in communities more exposed to modern life, traditional clothes are worn as Sunday best for church.

Women spend much of their leisure time embroidering. Sewing techniques have been passed down from previous generations. The patterns, colors, and fabrics of traditional costumes differ from region to region.

Leisure activities in the villages are usually centered around the family and the village community. Sunday afternoons are devoted to village dances, either in the village square or on specially-built platforms. A typical dance is the *hora* (HOR-rah), where participants gather around holding each other's shoulders and dance in a series of easy steps to the accompaniment of music. Food and drink are plentiful, as the women of the village get together to cook for the event. Leisure time is also spent on crafts such as embroidery, pottery, woodcarving, and quilt-making.

In rural communities, popular folktales are kept alive and passed on to the younger generation by word of mouth rather than through books. A typical folktale contains a moral or reflects aspects of human nature. Hence the traditional customs or culture and the wisdom of the elders in these close-knit communities are passed on to the young by storytelling.

URBAN LEISURE

The material conditions of life have been so harsh in Romania for so many years that most people living in urban centers have little time for leisure. Making money is a full-time activity, and hours that are available outside of work are often spent engaged on practical activities like home improvements or repairing the family car. With the large increases in prices that have taken place since the withdrawal of food subsidies, there has been a growing tendency for urban people to visit the countryside as much as possible where, in return for working in the fields of a relative's farm, locally grown food can be taken back to the city.

The little real leisure time that is available is spent going for a walk in a park or having a family picnic. Romanians also enjoy a game of

Romanian children are encouraged to play chess from an early age. Chess is thought to have been invented in India in the sixth century A.D. and was brought to Europe by the Arabs. The game became extremely popular in aristocratic circles as the tournaments and power struggles in medieval Europe could be enacted on the chessboard.

chess and listening to music. Visiting the cinema to catch Western films, which were rare before 1989, is a popular pastime. Although ticket prices are affordable by Western standards, for most Romanians a movie costs at least half a day's salary, thus they go to the movies only if something special is showing.

Watching television occupies a large portion of many people's free time. Before 1989 there were two channels, and one of these virtually closed down in 1985 as it was restricted to only two hours of cultural programs a day. The content of the main channel included news programs and patriotic songs, with politically correct dramas and documentaries about increasing productivity in factories. Romania now has several television channels, both public and private, and cable and satellite television. Antenna 1 is Romania's first commercial network and offers a wide variety of programs. Pro-TV is one of the most popular local channels, while teenagers and hip Romanians catch the latest music videos on Atomic TV. Lack of funding has seen many of Romania's television stations come under Western control. This has led to a flood of Western programming, not all of it good quality, being broadcast in Romania.

Radio has also changed since the introduction of private radio stations. One of the first to be established was Radio Fun, helped by Belgium's private radio station of the same name. Radio Contact, based in Bucharest, broadcasts the news in English and plays Western pop music and some Romanian music.

Before the revolution, newspapers in Romania were characterized by their dullness and predictability. Although there was more than one newspaper, the news was exactly the same except for the sports coverage that had a degree of independent reporting. Censorship meant that a uniform version of home and international news was presented to everyone on radio and television. In recent years there has been an increase in the number of newspapers and magazines available to Romanians, and there are more than half a dozen independent national papers. Minority-language newspapers are also available in some areas. The *Romaniai Magyar Szo* is the main Hungarian-language daily. The German *Deutsche Zeitung* is published weekly.

The political newspaper *Libertatea*. Magazines in foreign languages, such as English and French, can now be found in Bucharest today.

Ilie Nastase holding a copy of his biography *Nastase,* written by Richard Evans in 1978.

SPORTS

A very popular game played by young people mainly in the countryside is *oina* (OY-nah), a cross between baseball and cricket. The game is played on a field. The ball is thrown by a player on one team and hit with a bat by the opposing team. In schools, soccer and basketball are played by boys, while girls prefer gymnastics.

Local soccer teams from Bucharest qualify for European competitions regularly. The Romanian national soccer team is training for the 2006 FIFA World Cup competition. Romania's gymnasts have a long history of winning in the Olympics and in other international competitions. Gheorghe Muresan, a former Washington Bullets player, remains the only Romanian to play in the National Basketball Association (NBA) in the United States. But he has inspired many Romanian children to take up the sport. Tennis is also played in Romania. Ilie Nastase, the country's most successful tennis star, won the Masters championship four times (1972–75), and was a Wimbledon finalist in 1972 and 1976.

The fall of communism, however, has led to a decline in state funding and involvement in sports. Even gymnastics is struggling to finance its development. But many Romanians still turn to sports because of national pride and for self fulfilment. Outdoor activities such as hiking, cycling, exploring caves, and fishing are popular in Romania. Along the Black Sea coast, Romanians indulge in canoeing and other water sports.

NADIA COMANECI

The greatest Romanian gymnast was born in 1961 in Onesti, an industrialized city in Moldavia. When 6-year-old Comaneci was in school one day, the gymnastics scout, Bela Karolyi (later the Romanian gymnastics coach), looking for new recruits, asked "Who likes gymnastics?" Comaneci expressed interest and was given lessons along with other girls. Karolyi soon noticed Comaneci's fine sense of balance and her fearlessness, and she was singled out for special training. She was the national junior champion at age 10.

In 1976, at Madison Square Garden in New York, she became the first athlete to score a "10" at the annual American Cup International Gymnastics Competition. In the same year, she achieved perfect scores at the Montreal Olympics. Comaneci is the first woman to perform the double back somersault as a dismount from the uneven parallel bars. In Montreal, the reigning champion

was Olga Korbut of Russia, but she was ousted by the young Romanian who scored three 10s, a perfect score. No one had ever before been awarded such a score in the history of gymnastics in the Olympic Games and to obtain three was astonishing. By the end of the Games, the five-foot (1.53 m) tall Comaneci had won three gold medals, one silver, and one bronze.

Comaneci married U.S. Olympic champion Bart Connors in 1996 and they run several business operations. Comaneci was the first athlete to speak at the United Nations in 1999 when she launched the Year 2000 International Year of Volunteers program. In 2004, Comaneci began setting up a charity children's clinic in Bucharest that will care for orphans and children in her homeland.

FESTIVALS

ROMANIA HAS A RICH store of festivals that includes deeply religious events, such as Easter, and ancient secular ones originating in the country's pagan past. It is mainly in the countryside that traditional festivals and celebrations are observed. In different parts of the country, even within different towns in the same region, the various communities have their unique way of celebrating key moments in a year.

Left: **Folk dancing is an integral part of all Romanian festivals. This dance celebrates the harvest season.**

Opposite: **Romanian villagers gather for a religious ceremony.**

117

An outdoor church service in Marmures County on a beautiful winter day testifies to the fact that religion is an intimate part of life in rural Romania.

CHRISTMAS AND THE NEW YEAR

The first event in Romania's Christmas and New Year celebrations is Saint Nicholas' Day on December 6. Animals are slaughtered in preparation for the family feasts on this day. Young people begin their own preparations by resurrecting costumes or making new ones, and rehearsals begin for the *colinde* (CO-lin-deh), the singing of traditional songs outside people's homes on the night before Christmas to wish good luck for the new year.

In rural parts of Moldavia, a goat procession marks the end of one year and the beginning of another. The goat is depicted by a person suitably costumed to resemble the animal. Part of the facial mask includes a jaw socket that can be moved up and down to the accompaniment of music. The clacking sound that this movement produces represents the death pangs of the dying old year.

Another tradition at the end of the year involves a plow, decorated with green leaves to symbolize fertility and growth, being pulled from house to house and cutting a symbolic furrow in front of the family home to bring good luck and prosperity in the new year to the inhabitants. The ritual is done to the accompaniment of music; in Transylvania, a choir accompanies the plowers.

In northern Moldavia, January 1 is celebrated with the help of a special instrument that resembles an open barrel. It is drawn along the ground so as to make a loud sound, the significance of which has been lost over time. Sometimes the dragging of the barrel is accompanied by small troupes of players enacting mimes and dressed like bears and goats.

EASTER

Easter is the most important religious festival in Romania. The starting point is Palm Sunday, celebrating the day Jesus rode into Jerusalem on a donkey. On that day, small branches or pussy willows are distributed in churches and hung at home. The following week, the Week of Sufferings, and Lent, a period of 40 days prior to Good Friday, is an important time of devout prayer and fasting for Christians that simulates the time Jesus was preparing for his own death. While Good Friday remembers the crucifixion of Christ and is a solemn day, Easter Sunday is a joyful occasion, and every Christian church in the country is full of worshipers, particularly during midnight Mass.

Christians usually observe Easter on a Sunday in March or April, depending on the date of the first full moon after the spring equinox. The Eastern Orthodox Church follows the Julian rather than the Gregorian calendar, so Easter in Romania may be celebrated a month apart from Easter in other parts of the world.

MARTISOR

Martisor (MAR-tsi-shor) literally means March, and it is the name of an old custom to greet the coming of spring that is still observed in various parts of the country. On March 1, women are presented with simple and inexpensive amulets by men. Although similar to St. Valentine's Day in this respect, the gifts do not necessarily have romantic overtones. The little trinkets, tied with red and white strings—red symbolizes strength, wealth, health, and love; white symbolizes faith, hope, and purity—and worn as a brooch are an expression of friendship and represent good luck for the future.

SPRING AND SUMMER FESTIVALS

Easter is associated with pagan festivals celebrating the end of winter and the rebirth of a new year. Across Romania there are many celebrations of spring and summer that are not associated with religion, although in the last two decades of the Ceausescu era the intense process of urbanization destroyed many of the rural traditions that marked the end of winter.

One of the festivals that has survived is the Pageant of the Juni, held in the city of Brasov in Transylvania on the first Sunday of May. The word *juni* is from the Latin for young men, and the festival is based around parades of the city's young males dressed in their finest clothes and riding through the city to the accompaniment of a loud brass band. The parades set off from the steps of an old church in the heart of the old historic part of the city. At the end of the procession there is a public feast and more dancing and singing.

The antiquity of the Pageant of the Juni may be gauged from the fact that some of the costumes worn have been preserved by families for many generations, and in some cases, go back to the first half of the 19th century. One famous shirt worn in the procession has been sewn with over 4,000 spangles and weighs nearly 22 pounds (10 kg)!

The summer festival of *Sinzienele* (sin-ZI-air-nair-leh) is celebrated throughout rural Romania, though each region has its own specific ceremony and rituals. However, they have a common trait: the women gather flowers, leaves, and roots for medicinal use, and also to lure love, wealth, and luck, and to chase away evil spirits. *Sinzienele* occurs near the summer solstice.

THE SHEEP FEAST

This is a traditional shepherd's folk feast associated with the annual moving of the herds to the high pastures. There they graze under the watchful eyes of shepherds on the lookout for predators such as wolves. The sheep themselves do not belong to the shepherds but to the local inhabitants. A deal is negotiated with the shepherds, who not only guard the animals but also make cheeses for the villagers from the milk. An important part of the festival is the milking of sheep and the measuring of milk in order to ascertain the quantity of cheese to expect from each sheep.

A boy is dressed up in shepherd's clothes to act in a pageant that is part of the sheep festival.

The festivities vary according to district, but outdoor dances and shepherd-related activities are common features. For example, in some communities, the event opens with a performance known as the Dance of the Girls. The second stage of the festival is signalled by the oldest shepherd. There follows a lively scene as groups of men go through the motions of milking a flock of sheep and measuring out the milk into wooden pails. The men dress for the festival in waist-length sheepskin jackets that are decorated with embroidery and colored tassels. Body searches are playfully carried out to ensure that no one is secretly trying to obtain a higher rating by diluting their quota of milk with water.

After the event, the community feasts on cheese, local meat dishes, especially mutton, and plum brandy. The feast comes to an end with a display of folk dancing and singing.

Musicians coming together for the Songs of the Olt festival.

MUSIC FESTIVALS

Under Communist rule classical music was heavily subsidized by the state, so every large town had its own orchestra and full-time conductor. As in the case of sports, parents were keen to encourage any musical talent that their children might possess because this was one of the few ways a young Romanian could leave the country.

Romania has two major classical music festivals named in honor of Dinu Lipatti, a deceased pianist of the mid-20th century, and Gheorghe Enescu, the country's most famous composer and conductor. The Dinu Lipatti International Piano Competition is held during the month of May and takes place in a different city each year. The Gheorghe Enescu International Festival is held in Bucharest every three years.

Folk music festivals are more common and are organized in all parts of the country throughout the year, especially in August to coincide with harvest festivals. One of the biggest festivals, known as the Songs of the Olt, takes place in the town of Calimanesti in Walachia.

THE *CALUSARII*

The *calusarii* (kah-loo-SHA-ree), also known as the *calusul* (kah-loo-SOO), is the name of the dance that forms part of the ritual of Calus, associated with the town of Calarasi (KA-LA-RA-SHI), which is about 100 miles (260 km) west of Bucharest, on the Danube. This dance and its associated rites go far back into the pagan past as part of a fertility and healing ritual. It is related to the world of magic, and a diminishing minority of followers still believe that if all the various rites are carefully and strictly carried out, then magic can indeed be performed.

Learning the dance steps took place in secret and was led by a village elder who had been instructed in the steps of the magical dance by his predecessor. Only an odd number of men, between five and nine, would be initiated, and this group of men would swear an oath to the group

and their leader to dance together for a number of years. At Whitsuntide, 50 days after Easter Sunday, the dancers would go from house to house, dancing and chanting various incantations. The costumed *calusarii* performers are led by a flag bearer and a masked "mute," who traditionally would wear a red phallus beneath his robes and mutter sexual incantations. In the past the mute apparently played a far greater role than that today, where he has been relegated to the role of the buffoon. The mute carries a sword while the rest carry sticks that they would beat and wave in a rhythmic manner, unaccompanied by musicians. The performers bless each household with children and a bountiful harvest and heal those who are ill.

The *calusarii* is still practiced in a dwindling number of communities in southern Romania. But most times nowadays, the dance is performed by dance troupes at annual celebrations or for tourists without its corresponding rituals and magical symbolism.

FOOD

OVER THE LAST 10 years of Ceausescu's regime, food was a precious commodity in Romania. Obtaining sufficient food for daily meals was a major preoccupation for most people. The situation has slowly changed since 1989, but even though more food is available in shops and restaurants, it is often so costly that few people can afford it. Despite its high price, more meat is now consumed than ever before. This is probably a reaction to the years of deprivation that are still vividly remembered.

Opposite: **A woman sells home prepared spices in a market in the town of Baia Mare.**

Below: **Preparing** *tocana* **(a rich soup) and making bread for the evening meal are usually done by Romanian women.**

FOLK DISHES

Mamaliga (mah-me-LI-ga) is the staple food of Romanians in all parts of the country, and in the countryside it is eaten cold for breakfast. It is a thick mush made from corn that is served in a variety of ways. Corn was imported into Europe from America where Native Americans had cultivated it for centuries, and it reached Romania in the second half of the 19th century. *Mamaliga* is traditionally prepared with a *facalet* (fah-KEH-letz), a wooden stick somewhat like a rolling pin with the top sometimes carved with an individual design and the owner's name. Another important staple food in Romania is bread.

The best dishes in Romania come from the countryside. Romania can boast a number of traditional dishes that would be far more common if meat was more readily obtainable. *Tocana* (tok-CANA), which means stew, is like a borsch soup and is a very popular meal in rural areas. The usual meat used is chicken or mutton, and *tocana* is flavored with onions and garlic. Vegetables in the stew include potatoes, carrots, peppers, and beans. It is still the practice just before winter in rural areas to bury vegetables in a deep hole in the ground that is covered with leaves and straw. When snow falls, the vegetables are preserved until early spring.

Pork mixed with beef, or sometimes lamb, is also used to make grilled meatballs known as *mititei* (me-tee-TAY), a word that comes from the word for small. They resemble small hamburgers or are cylindrical in shape and have a spicier taste. By tradition

A dish of *sarmale*.

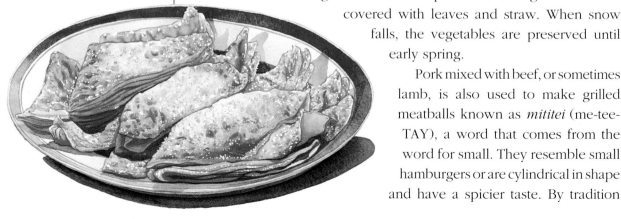

they are broiled outdoors over charcoal and served hot with red or green peppers and sour pickles flavored with dill. *Mititei* is often eaten as a snack or as an appetizer with mustard and is consumed with a glass of wine or beer. *Mititei* is sold by street vendors in the cities.

Ciorba (CHOR-ba) is a sour soup, with the traditional sour base made from the fermented juice of wheat bran. It takes time to prepare the soup, and nowadays Romanians tend to use unripened green grapes, green sorrel leaves, or lemon juice, instead of fermenting wheat bran.

Sarmale (sar-MALL-eh), a dish of Armenian and Greek origin, is very popular throughout the country. It consists of cabbage or grape leaves stuffed with rice, meat, and herbs. The filling can be cooked in tomato or lemon sauce, and *sarmale* is sometimes served with cream.

The most common desserts in Romania are pancakes and *placinte* (pla-CHIN-te), which are like crepe suzettes or turnovers in North America. The Turkish influence on Romanian food is apparent in the fondness for baklava, a pastry with crushed pistachios or almonds glazed with thick syrup served as a dessert.

Torte (TOHRT), a variety of rich cake, is becoming more common since the ingredients are more easily available. It used to be made by young village girls who took turns meeting at one of their kitchens on a Sunday afternoon to make the dessert together.

THE FOOD HASSLE OF OLD

During the four months of summer, the markets in every Romanian town and city are filled with vegetables and fruits. Carrots, cabbage, corn, cherries, and strawberries are in plentiful supply. This used to be the only time of the year when lining up to purchase food was not necessary.

Until recently, the situation in the winter was very different. Fresh vegetables were mostly unobtainable, and items like bread and cheese were scarce. A standard meal for many families was a thin broth made from rice and chicken or pig's bones.

Shopping for food was a demoralizing experience. Not only were standard items frequently rationed, but the shortage of basic foodstuffs encouraged and maintained a widespread black market. It was common practice for staff in food shops to keep some food off the shelves and sell them later when supplies were no longer available. Hence, the staff were able to command a higher price by selling the foodstuffs in the black market.

Menus in restaurants may list half a dozen different meals, but in reality only one might be available because the ingredients were simply not obtainable. The only people who could have full meals regularly were groups of tourists on package tours who stayed at special tourist hotels. The reality of the food situation was kept hidden from them. At the time, Romania was exporting large quantities of food in an attempt to pay off the country's accumulated foreign debts. Meat was often obtainable only through the black market, and the only Romanians who could eat well were high-ranking members of the government.

DRINK

Tuica (TSUI-kuh), a brandy usually made from plums, is the national alcoholic drink. A glass is customarily drunk neat, without adding water or fruit juice, before meals and at festivities. At weddings, *tuica* is often the main drink. Sometimes it is made from pears and other fruits. In Transylvania, *palinca* (pal-INK-ka) is the Hungarian equivalent of *tuica*. It is distilled twice and is far more potent.

The Romanian rural equivalent of a bar where alcohol is drunk is sometimes called a *circiuma* (kr-CHU-ma).

Romania has a long tradition in wine-growing. It is said that in the 19th century, Polish princes used to buy Romanian wines and escorted the wine back to Poland with drawn swords as though they were transporting gold. Wines from the Murfatlar region in southeastern Romania have won many European wine awards. Generally, a bottle of wine is not very expensive in Romania.

Coffee is far more popular than tea. The reason for the popularity of coffee may be the legacy of Turkey's historical influence over the country. Coffee is usually drunk black and very sweet, as is the custom in Turkey.

Tuica, or Romanian plum brandy.

CIORBA OF VEAL

Ciorba is a sour soup made traditionally with the fermented juice from wheat bran. Lemon juice can be substituted for the wheat bran.

1 veal shank
2 cups water
Salt to taste
$^1/_4$ pound (113 g) butter
3 onions, sliced
1 shallot, sliced
1 cup diced potatoes
1 cup diced celery
Lemon juice
2 sprigs parsley, chopped
Sour cream

Cut the meat into small pieces and boil slowly in water. Add salt to taste. Meanwhile, melt the butter in a pan and sauté the onions and shallot. Add diced vegetables and stir for a minute.

When the veal is almost tender, add the vegetable mix into the soup and leave the soup to simmer. When cooked, remove from heat, add lemon juice, and garnish with the parsley. Serve in bowls with a dab of sour cream on top.

PLACINTE CU MERE (APPLE STRUDEL)

It has been claimed that all Romanian women know how to bake a good apple strudel.

2 pounds (1 kg) apples
2–3 tablespoons water
$^1/_2$ cup (240 g) sugar
1 teaspoon ground cinnamon
Strudel dough
Butter to grease the pan
2 tablespoons soft butter for greasing the dough
Confectioner's sugar with vanilla flavor

Peel the apples and then grate with a vegetable grater or slice thinly. Boil the apples with 2 to 3 tablespoons of water, stirring continuously until the apples have softened. Add the sugar and boil until the mixture becomes a paste. Remove from the heat and let the paste cool. Add the cinnamon when the paste is cold.

Cut the strudel dough into pieces the size of the baking pan. Grease individually 6 or 7 pieces of strudel dough, then place in the greased pan. Spread the dough with the apple paste. Cover with 6 or 7 pieces of individually greased strudel dough one on top of the other. Grease the top layer of dough. Bake at 350°F (177°C) until golden brown. When the pie is done, cut into squares and sprinkle with the vanilla sugar.

MAP OF ROMANIA

ECONOMIC ROMANIA

Agriculture

Grain

Livestock

Wine

Services

Airport

Port

Tourism

Manufacturing

Food Products

Paper Products

Ship Building

Textiles

Wood Products

Natural Resources

Coal

Fish

Oil

Salt

Timber

ABOUT THE ECONOMY

OVERVIEW
Farming, fishing, forestry, and mining have been the mainstay of Romania's economy for centuries. Oil refining, and heavy and light industries are major sectors. Tourism and the service industry are growing in importance.

GROSS DOMESTIC PRODUCT (GDP)
$155 billion (2003)

GDP SECTORS
Services 45.2 percent; industry 43.2 percent; agriculture 11.6 percent (2003)

LAND AREA
91,700 square miles (237,500 square km)

WORKFORCE
9.9 million (2002)

WORKFORCE BY OCCUPATION
Agriculture 41.4 percent; industry 27.3 percent; services 31.3 percent (2000)

CURRENCY
Romania leu (ROL) (plural: lei)
Notes: 1000, 2000, 5000, 10,000, 50,000, 100,000 lei
Coins: 100, 500 lei
USD 1 = ROL 30,352 (November 2004)

INFLATION RATE
12.3 percent (May 2004)

UNEMPLOYMENT RATE
6.5 percent (2003 estimate)

NATURAL RESOURCES
Gold, silver, salt, natural gas, oil, coal, lignite, iron, manganese, feldspar, pyrite, marble, graphite, bauxite, mica, timber

AGRICULTURAL PRODUCTS
Corn, wheat, barley, sugar beets, sunflower seeds, potatoes, grapes, dairy products, fruit, fish

INDUSTRIAL PRODUCTS
Textiles, footwear, paper, machinery and vehicles, wood products, construction materials, metallurgy, chemicals, food, petroleum, plastics

MAJOR TRADE PARTNERS
European Union, the United Kingdom, the United States, the Russian Federation

MAJOR EXPORTS
Textiles, footwear, metals and metal products, machinery and equipment, minerals, fuel

MAJOR IMPORTS
Machinery and equipment, fuel, minerals, chemicals, textiles

MAJOR PORTS
Constanta

CULTURAL ROMANIA

Sighet Prison
During Communist times, the Sighet Prison in Sighetu Maramatiei was known as the Prison of the Ministers for its political inmates. Now empty of its prisoners, it reopened in 1997 as the Memorial Museum of the Victims of Communism and Anti-Communist Resistance.

Sucevita Monastery
Built by the princes Simion and Ieremia Movila between 1582 and 1584, the massive, fortified Sucevita Monastery in Moldavia is famous for the vivid frescoes that cover much of its interior. The tombs of the monastery's founders lie within. During Communist rule, only nuns over 50 were allowed to stay at the monastery.

Baile Herculane
Legend has it that Hercules bathed in the springs here to heal the wounds caused by the Hydra. The first baths were built by Roman legions after their conquest of the Dacians and in the 19th century, Baile Herculane in Caras Severin became a fashionable resort.

Danube delta
The Danube delta has the largest reed beds in the world and a large population of wildlife. Hundreds of migratory and native birds nest on the delta, including endangered species such as the great white egret and the white-tailed eagle, making the delta an excellent place for bird-watching.

Apuseni Mountains
The Apuseni Mountains in the Western Carpathians are renowned for their extensive cave systems lined with large limestone formations. The Cetatile Ponorului is one of the most impressive cave systems. Carved by a river, it cuts through an entire mountain, creating a natural bridge.

Sighisoara
Settled by the Saxons in the 12th century, Sighisoara in Wallachia is considered the most complete site of medieval architecture in Romania. Much of the old town or citadel is in good condition and nine of the original 14 towers remain. Vlad Tepes of Dracula legend was born in Sighisoara around 1431.

Retezat National Park
Located in Hunedoara in the south-western Transylvania Carpathians, the country's first national park and a UNESCO Biosphere Reserve is home to around 300 plant species and numerous animals, such as the brown bear, wolf, fox, and deer.

Palace of Parliament
Located in Bucharest, the Palace of Parliament is the second largest building in the world in surface area and is a massive example of Ceausescu's megalomania in the 1980s. It is 885 feet by 787 feet (270 m by 240 m) and 282 feet (86 m) high, with a surface area of 3.6 million square feet (330,000 square m).

Tropaeum Traiani
Near the town of Adamclisi is a reconstruction of the Tropaeum Traiani. The original monument was built in A.D.106–9 to commemorate Trajan's conquest of the Dacians. Scenes from the battle are depicted at the base.

ABOUT THE CULTURE

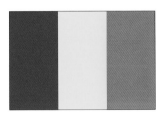

COUNTRY NAME
Romania

CAPITAL
Bucharest

OTHER MAJOR CITIES
Brasov, Cluj-Napoca, Constanta, Iasi, Timisoara

GOVERNMENT
Republic

POPULATION
22,271,839 (2003)

COUNTIES AND MUNICIPALITIES
Alba, Arad, Arges, Bacau, Bihor, Bistrita-Nasaud, Botosani, Braila, Brasov, Bucharest (Municipality), Buzau, Calarasi, Caras-Severin, Cluj, Constanta, Covasna, Dimbovita, Dolj, Galati, Giurgiu, Gorj, Harghita, Hunedoara, Ialomita, Iasi, Ilfov, Maramures, Mehedinti, Mures, Neamt, Olt, Prahova, Salaj, Satu Mare, Sibiu, Suceava, Teleorman, Timis, Tulcea, Vaslui, Vilcea, Vrancea

NATIONAL FLAG
Three vertical bands of cobalt blue, chrome yellow, and vermilion red

NATIONAL ANTHEM
Awaken Thee, Romanian! (*Desteapta-te, Romane!*). It was originally a poem written by Andrei Muresan at the time of the 1848 revolution. The music was composed by Anton Pann.

ETHNIC GROUPS
Romanian 89.5 percent, Hungarian 6.6 percent, Roma 2.5 percent, Ukrainian 0.3 percent, German 0.3 percent, Russian 0.2 percent, Turkish 0.2 percent, other 0.4 percent (2002)

RELIGIONS
Eastern Orthodox 87 percent, Protestant 6.8 percent, Catholic 5.6 percent, other 0.4 percent

OFFICIAL LANGUAGE
Romanian

LITERACY RATE
98.4 percent (2003)

NATIONAL HOLIDAYS
New Year (January 1 and 2), Easter Monday (March/April), Unification Day (December 1), Christmas (December 25 and 26).

LEADERS IN POLITICS
Carol I—prince (1866–81), king (1881–1914)
Gheorghe Gheorghiu-Dej—general secretary (1947–65)
Nicolae Ceausescu—president (1965–89)
Ion Iliescu—president (1989–96, 2000–04)
Emil Constantinescu—president (1996–2000)
Adrian Nastase—prime minister (2000–04)

TIME LINE

IN ROMANIA	IN THE WORLD
	753 B.C. Rome is founded.
700 B.C. The Dacian civilization develops.	
	116–17 B.C. The Roman Empire reaches its greatest extent, under Emperor Trajan (98–17).
A.D. 106 The Romans conquer Dacia.	
A.D. 600–900 The Slavs and Magyars move into Dacia.	**A.D. 600** Height of Mayan civilization
	1000 The Chinese perfect gunpowder and begin to use it in warfare.
1003 Transylvania becomes a part of the Hungarian kingdom.	
1330 The state of Walachia is formed.	
1359 Moldavia achieves independence.	
1434 Ottoman Empire advances into Dacia.	**1530** Beginning of trans-Atlantic slave trade organized by the Portuguese in Africa.
1600 Michael the Brave briefly unites Walachia, Moldavia, and Transylvania. The next year Romania is formally recognized as a state.	**1558–1603** Reign of Elizabeth I of England
	1620 Pilgrims sail the *Mayflower* to America.
1699 Transylvania comes under the Habsburg kingdom.	
1711 Greek Phanariot rule begins.	**1776** U.S. Declaration of Independence
	1789–99 The French Revolution
1859 Alexandru Cuzu is elected ruler of both Moldavia and Walachia.	**1861** The U.S. Civil War begins.

IN ROMANIA	IN THE WORLD
1866	
First Romanian constitution is created.	**1869**
1877	The Suez Canal is opened.
Romania formally becomes independent.	
1881	
Romania is recognized as a kingdom.	**1914**
1920	World War I begins.
Transylvania is returned to Romania.	**1939**
1940	World War II begins.
Northern Transylvania is ceded to Hungary and other territories to the Soviet Union.	
1945	**1945**
Soviet-backed government is installed.	The United States drops atomic bombs on Hiroshima and Nagasaki.
1947	
Romania regains Tranyslvania.	**1949**
Romanian People's Republic is established.	The North Atlantic Treaty Organization (NATO) is formed.
1955	**1957**
Romania joins the Warsaw Pact.	The Russians launch Sputnik.
	1966–69
	The Chinese Cultural Revolution
1985–86	**1986**
Nicolae Ceausescu implements austerity program.	Nuclear power disaster at Chernobyl in Ukraine
1989	
Ceausescu is deposed and executed.	
1990	
First elections are held.	**1991**
Ion Iliescu becomes president.	Break-up of the Soviet Union
	1997
2000	Hong Kong is returned to China.
Cyanide devastates the Danube.	**2001**
Ion Iliescu is reelected as president.	Terrorists crash planes in New York, Washington, D.C., and Pennsylvania.
2003	**2003**
Referendum held on new constitution	War in Iraq
2004	
Romania joins NATO.	

GLOSSARY

buchium (BU-chium)
Alpenhorn used by shepherds to communicate, now considered a musical instrument.

calusarii (KAH-loo-SHA-ree)
A dance associated with magic.

cirque (CHIRK)
Steep, hollow excavations on mountainsides made by glacial erosion.

colinde (CO-lin-deh)
Traditional songs expressing good luck for the new year that are sung outside homes on Christmas Eve.

collectivization
The ownership and control of the means of production and distribution is given to the people involved instead of a few individuals.

Dacians
Earliest recorded inhabitants, colonized by the Romans between the first and fourth centuries.

Eastern Orthodox Church
A group of churches that recognizes the jurisdiction of the Patriarch of Constantinople; believers of the Eastern Orthodox Church follow the teachings of the church before the schism in the 11th century.

iconostasis
A decorated screen in Eastern Orthodox churches that separates the sanctuary from the nave.

kontra-violin (KON-tra)
An instrument similar to the viola, but with only three strings.

Magyars
Ethnic Hungarians who originated in Central Asia.

mamaliga (mah-me-LI-ga)
Staple food made from cornmeal.

Phanariots
Greek nobles sent by the Turks to rule Romania in the 18th century.

Tatars
People belonging to the various Mongolian and Turkic tribes, who under Genghis Khan (1162–1227) and his successors ruled parts of central and western Asia and eastern Europe until the 18th century.

transubstantiation
Eastern Orthodox church belief that during Holy Communion the substance of bread and wine becomes the body and blood of Christ, with only the appearance of bread and wine remaining.

tuica (TSUI-kuh)
A type of brandy usually made from plums.

voivodates
Areas under the control of a military leader known as a voivode.

FURTHER INFORMATION

BOOKS

Bryan, Nichol. *Danube: Cyanide Spill*. Environmental Disasters Series. Cleveland, OH: World Almanac, 2003.

Cipkowski, Peter. *Revolution in Eastern Europe: Understanding the Collapse of Communism in Poland, Hungary, East Germany, Czechoslovakia, Romania and the Soviet Union*. New York, NY: John Wiley & Sons, 1991.

Greenley, August. *Man-made Disasters: Toxic waste: Chemical spills in our world*. New York, NY: The Rosen Publishing Group, Inc., 2003.

Klepper, Nicholae. *Romania: An illustrated history*. Illustrated Histories Series. New York, NY: Hippocrene Books, 2003.

Oprea, Tiberiu. *Romania*. Countries of the World Series. Milwaukee, WI: Gareth Stevens, 2003.

Popseu, Julian. *Romania*. Major World Nations Series. Langhorne, PA: Chelsea House, 2000.

Rady, Martyn C.. *Collapse of Communism in Eastern Europe: Causes and Consequences*. Austin, TX: Raintree/Steck Vaughn, 1995.

Roman, Radu Anton and Radu Langu. *Bucharest*. New York, NY: Parkstone Press, 1999.

Sharp, Anne Wallace. *The Gypsies*. San Diego, CA: Lucent Books, 2002.

Spariosu, Mihai and Dezso Bendek. *Ghosts, vampires and werewolves: Eerie tales from Transylvania*. New York, NY: Orchard Books, 1994.

Willis, Terri. *Romania*. Enchantment of the World Second Series. New York, NY: Children's Press, 2001.

VIDEOS

100 Years of Lies: Short documentary on the Romanian castle of Bran, known as Dracula's Castle. C21ETV, 1999. (VHS)

Children Underground. New Video Group, 2003. (DVD)

Fall of Communism. MPI Home Video, 2002. (DVD)

WEBSITES

Central Intelligence Agency World Factbook (select "Romania" from the country list)
www.cia.gov/cia/publications/factbook

Embassy of Romania in Washington D.C. www.roembus.org

Romanian National Tourist Office. www.romaniatourism.com/location.html

U.S. Department of State Background Notes (select "Romania" from the country list)
www.state.gov/r/pa/ei/bgn

BIBLIOGRAPHY

ANEIR–Foreign Trade Promotion Center. www.aneir-cpce.ro

Brinkle, Lydle. *Hippocrene Companion Guide to Romania*. New York: Hippocrene Books, 1992.

Burford, Tim and Dan Richardson. *Rough Guide to Romania (third edition)*. London: Rough Guides Limited, 2001.

Central Intelligence Agency World Factbook. www.cia.gov/cia/publications/factbook/geos/ro.html

Country Profile: Romania (1993/1994). Economist Intelligence Unit, London, November 1993.

Eliade, Mircea. *The Romanians: A concise history*. Bucharest, Romania: Roza Vinturilor Publishing House, 1992.

Embassy of Romania in Washington D.C. www.roembus.org

Energy Information Administration (U.S. Department of Energy) www.eia.doe.gov/emeu/cabs/romaenv.html

Government of Romania. www.gov.ro/engleza

Kemp, Cathryn and Steve Kokker. *Lonely Planet: Romania & Moldova (third edition)*. Melbourne, Australia: Lonely Planet Publications, 2004.

Parliament of Romania. www.cdep.ro/pls/dic/site-page?id=103&idl=2

Romania Factbook 2000. www.factbook.net

The Agency for Governmental Strategies. *Explore Romania 2003*. Bucharest, Romania: Agency for Governmental Strategies, 2003.

World Wildlife Fund. www.panda.org

INDEX